MAKING THEIR LUCK

The Zetmeir Family in Bavaria and America

Karl David Zetmeir

authorHOUSE®

AuthorHouse™
1663 Liberty Drive
Bloomington, IN 47403
www.authorhouse.com
Phone: 833-262-8899

Published by AuthorHouse 04/08/2021

ISBN: 978-1-6655-2138-3 (sc)
ISBN: 978-1-6655-2136-9 (hc)
ISBN: 978-1-6655-2137-6 (e)

Print information available on the last page.

DEDICATION

This book would not have been possible without the help of others. The contributions of so many family members over the years are acknowledged and appreciated. I therefore respectfully dedicate this book to all the "storytellers" in our family who have lived, loved, struggled, endured, and worked to "make their own luck."

Whatsoever you do, do it heartily, as to the Lord, and not unto men. Knowing that of the Lord, you will receive the reward of the inheritance: for you serve the Lord Christ.
-Colossians 3:23-24 KJV

"If I only work hard enough, I'll make my own luck."

-Les Zetmeir, 1920-2005

Karl David Zetmeir
Lieutenant Colonel, US Army (Retired)
Leavenworth, Kansas
2021

CONTENTS

The Zetmeir Family, Emporia, Kansas, circa 1889.

THE JOURNEY

MY INTEREST IN OUR FAMILY history really began when I was just a kid. I loved asking my folks for stories about the times in which they had lived. Because my father was a particularly good storyteller, our family trips were filled with his funny anecdotes and stories about his life growing up in Topeka, Kansas. They were about how they lived through the Great Depression, going to school, playing sports, his parents, siblings, relatives, working conditions, the railroads, the war, their neighbors and just everything about that time seemed to make cracking good stories that kept us entertained for hours. We knew of course, that our surname was German, but other than hearing they had come from somewhere around Munich, nobody knew for sure if that was true or not, or even when my great-grandparents had arrived in America.

As a result, my interest in our family's German past stayed with me as I grew up. I studied German language in high school and even joined the high school German Club. When I graduated from North Kansas City High School in 1977, I enlisted in the US Army to be a Military Policeman. Even my choice of service was based in part at least, on the chance to be stationed in Germany and see the land of our heritage. After serving my first year in Virginia, I got my chance in March 1979 when I was reassigned to the US Army's Berlin Brigade. It was in West Berlin that I met my future wife; Manuela Brümmer. Her family had fled East Berlin in 1961 just before the communist East Germans divided the city with the infamous Berlin Wall. Manuela spoke no English at the time and my paltry two years of high school German hardly made me a linguist, but it at least gave us a foundation to communicate.

 1

I had met Manuela in the last four months of my three-year Berlin tour. In fact, I already had orders to go to California, so in 1982 I had to leave Berlin and Manuela for what became a lonely one-year assignment to Fort Hunter-Liggett, California. During that year, we maintained our relationship through letters and monthly phone calls. In April 1983, the US Army responded to an upswing in the terrorist threat in Europe by ordering an increased number of military policemen to be sent to Germany at once. Though I had already served a three-year tour in Berlin and had been back in the states less than a year, I was nevertheless identified as one of those to be transferred. To say the least, it was an incredibly happy Sergeant Zetmeir who received orders to transfer back to Germany, this time for duty with the 3rd Armored Division in Butzbach, a small town in the German state of Hessen near Frankfurt. I arrived in April 1983 and Manuela and I were both happy to be reunited. Verbal communication was still challenging, but I embarked on a rigorous language self-study effort and learned a lot very quickly. At least for the first years of our marriage, German would become our primary language and remain an integral part of our lives forever.

Manuela and I were married in Butzbach, Germany on 6 October 1983. As we later discovered, this was almost 100 years to the month since my great grandfather, Joseph Zehetmeier, had immigrated to America. After our wedding ceremony and a brief honeymoon in the Netherlands, we moved Manuela's household things along with her four-year old daughter Sonja from Berlin to Butzbach and our new family was started.

The idea of actually researching our family genealogy began on a kind of lark. My folks Les and Colleen in Kansas City had been unable to attend our wedding in Germany, so in 1984 they decided to visit us in Butzbach to meet their new German daughter-in-law and granddaughter. I decided that I would simply use the time prior to their arrival to find out where in Germany our family had come from. That way, or so I reasoned at the time, we could all visit our city of origin together. I recall thinking that finding our home city could not be all that difficult a task. As it turned out, I was completely wrong about that.

I went to our base library and found the one book they had on genealogy entitled: 'Finding Your Roots' by Jeanne Westin. I became fascinated with the book and it became my genealogy bible for the next few years. I soon discovered that Germany had no central national archives for genealogical research. All birth, marriage and death records were kept in local city and church archives. So, in a kind of Catch-22, I learned that to conduct successful genealogical research in Germany, one had to already *know* the city of origin as the start point. Adding to the problem was that I was in Germany, and the family relatives that might know more about the Zetmeir city of origin and birthplaces were all back in the United States. I began a long-distance mail and phone call campaign to relatives and various archives in America. My hope was to find a document that might provide a birthplace or marriage record so I could then know where to dig for more of our history. This all started in 1984, and I had a deadline as my three-year tour of duty would end in May of 1986.

Using the Westin book as a guide, I began writing letters to my parents, aunts and uncles for anything they might know about where in Germany our family had started. Unfortunately, nobody in the family seemed to know the exact town or region from which our family came. Some said they had heard it was near Munich, others said they were from the Baden-Baden area (Joseph Zehetmeier's obit gives Baden-Baden as his birthplace, which put me on the wrong trail for months). But I sent letters to wherever I thought I might get some good information on the family. Genealogy, I learned, is not as much research as it is an actual investigation. It is truly detective work. And this was the pre-internet world. I wrote letters to relatives asking for locations in America where my great-grandparents had lived, to vital statistics bureaus for birth or death records, to newspapers for obituaries, to various archives in both the US and Germany for passenger manifests and paid professional genealogists to search records I could not access. In between, I made quite a lot of trans-Atlantic phone calls to family and archives as well.

After dozens of letters, lots of disappointments and two years after my parent's Germany visit, our big break came in 1986. The Vital

Statistics Bureau in Arkansas responded with the death certificate of my great-grandfather, Joseph Zetmeir. This turned out to be the most crucial document I would find. All the official records I had previously located on him had simply listed Germany as his birthplace. I found to my excitement that on Joseph's death certificate, his youngest daughter Mary Klug (as their certificate witness) had noted Joseph's city of birth as well as country. The document listed his birthplace as '*Unterbachling, Bavaria, Germany.*' Though badly misspelled, it took me no time to match it to the Bavarian city of *Unterhaching,* which was near Munich, just as our family lore had always maintained. Feeling like I had hit the jackpot, I quickly wrote to the Oklahoma Vital Statistics Bureau for my great-grandmother Magdalena's death certificate in the hope that Mary had likewise been her official witness as well. Within a few weeks, I received Magdalena Stangl's death certificate and found that Mary had indeed witnessed that document as well. Like the previous document, the birth city was misspelled as '*Holtzcharen, Germany,*' but it took no time to match it to the town of *Holzkirchen,* which was located to the south of Unterhaching. So the family elders back in the USA *had* been mostly correct after all. Joseph and Magdalena Zetmeir had indeed come from the area near Munich; the Bavarian cities of Unterhaching and Holzkirchen. Both cities were just to the south of Munich. I could at last begin researching in Germany proper. I had but a few months left on my tour to do this.

As is often the case in genealogy, the situation dictates that one must enlist the help of a professional. And I needed help to do get into the right archives in Munich. Months earlier, I had contracted with a German student named Reinhard Mayer at the University of Munich who did genealogy research on the side. He had made some inquiries on my behalf, but since we did not have a precise city of origin, nothing had come of it. Now, with their two birthplaces in hand, he quickly uncovered a veritable treasure trove of information about the Zetmeirs. In Unterhaching, he was able to quickly locate not only birth, marriage and death records, but located the addresses in Unterhaching where Joseph had lived at different times. Amazingly, he was able to dig through the city and church archives and collect information on our family for several generations back to around 1600. Family trees and group sheets that I had only been able to make a few entries on were now quickly filling up.

A few months later, Manuela and I drove from Butzbach to Unterhaching to meet with Reinhard Mayer. He had even taken the effort to coordinate with the owners for a tour of the very house at #21 Bergermeister-Prenn Strasse (today #2 Bergermeister-Prenn Str.) where my grandfather Joseph *Zehetmeier* had been born. The owners were very welcoming and gave us a thorough tour of the house and its adjoining farm. At that time, the house was still configured as the general goods store, farm, and blacksmith shop it had been for generations of owners since the days the *Zehetmeiers* had owned it. It was quite a feeling to finally be at this place. I had always joked that my height at six feet made me the shortest Zetmeir in the family. However, as I walked around the main floor, ducking below the ceilings that were barely over six feet themselves, I was glad for it. Reinhard had also arranged for us to meet with Mr. Rudolf Felzmann, who was a local author and hobby historian in Unterhaching. An *Afrika Korps* veteran who had been a POW in the United States, he very much enjoyed meeting an American soldier. He was extremely interested in our *Zehetmeier* family research as it was part of the Unterhaching history as well. In true German style of business before pleasure, we compared our notes and exchanged information, before turning to a more leisurely discussion of soldierly things over coffee. He then graciously presented us with an autographed copy of his book *Unterhaching: Ein Heimatbuch,* on the history of Unterhaching.

This is where the story took a very unexpected turn. About a month after this visit to Unterhaching, I received a letter from a Mrs. Eva Barthel who lived in the town of Hohenschäftlarn, just west of Unterhaching. In her letter, she wrote that word had gotten around about a recent visit to Unterhaching of an American soldier who was researching his *Zehetmeier* family name. She explained that her maiden name was *Zehetmayr* and that her grandfather's brother had immigrated to America about one hundred years before. She inquired as to whether

I was indeed the American soldier she had heard about, and that if I was, asked me please write back to her. Her letter contained her phone number, so I called her and confirmed that I was indeed the Zetmeir she was looking for. During our conversation I could not help but ask how she had found my address in Butzbach as we lived in military quarters. We learned Eva had gone to the rather extreme effort of calling the United States Army-EUROPE (USAEUR) Headquarters in Heidelberg, Germany and inquired whether they had a soldier named Zetmeir. At first, the officials she talked with had cited operational security reasons and said they could not confirm any information about me. But Eva persisted with a convincingly tearful grandmotherly plea for them to please help her find what was probably "her only other living relative in the whole world." They then relented and gave her my name and German address in Butzbach. While that certainly does not say much for US Army operational security and privacy practices of the time, it was certainly a very fortuitous turn of events for our family story!

It was not long after that we arranged a weekend visit to Eva's home in Hohenschäftlarn. She had gone to the extra effort of contacting several other distant Zetmeir relatives and arranged for them to meet us for a small reunion of sorts. After we all gathered around her big dining table, Eva commenced to placing old black and white photographs on the table, announcing; "Now, THIS is your grandfather, and these are his children" and explained about how the photos had been sent to them from the Zetmeirs in America many years before. I recall not really knowing what to say, so I just opened my briefcase and began laying exact duplicates of each photo next to the ones she had placed on the table. Everyone in the room, us included, had goosebumps at that point and just looked at one another in amazement. Any lingering doubts about whether we were family or not quickly evaporated. We felt we had bridged the Atlantic! Our family connection thus confirmed, we spent the rest of our visit listening to them tell Zehetmeier family stories over beer and sausages while I furiously scribbled notes and struggled to keep up while focusing to understand, as did my Berliner Manuela, with their particularly challenging Bavarian dialect. It was so rewarding to have at last uncovered our family's point of origin in Germany and the bonus of finding and meeting distant relatives made it even more special. I had to laugh a bit as I recalled my original notion that finding our family's birthplace would be easy and only take a few months.

Our tour in Germany was about to end, but we were able to visit Eva one more time. On that visit, she gave me a few more photos and even an original letter my great-grandfather Joseph had written to his nephew Johann-Baptist Zehetmayr in Africa prior to World War I. She also talked about her own branch of our family tree in Germany, about what they had done and her life growing up as well. She even shared her personal *Stammbuch* containing entries of her other relatives. Unknown in the USA, *Stammbuch*s are small German family tree books given to brides at a wedding that contain blank entries for registering births, deaths and marriages. They are used like Americans traditionally used family bibles to do the same thing. In what proved a sobering moment, she showed me that each Zehetmeier entry bore a swastika stamp next to it. She explained during the Third Reich, every German was required to provide evidence of their 'racial purity' by presenting their *Stammbuchs* to the local Nazi officials. Having studied the Second World War for most of my life, it was very eerie to see our family name touched by this dark chapter of history.

Eva Barthel's home had many beautiful heirloom furniture pieces. I noticed one antique bookcase cabinet that had thick, hand-rolled glass doors: with and an unmistakable bullet hole in one of its panes. Eva told us that during the US military occupation of Bavaria in the aftermath the war, some US Constabulary soldiers had searched her home looking for contraband. They had also admired the beautiful cabinet with the thick glass doors and wondered aloud if its glass doors were bullet proof. So, one of them casually fired his M1 rifle, putting a hole through it and scaring Eva and her family out of their wits in the process. As the soldiers rummaged through their belongings, one of them came across some postcards with US postmarks. They were from Joseph and Magdalena in the states. Seeing the Kansas postmark on them, they declared since they had relatives in the USA, they must be "okay." They were never bothered again. As she showed us cards and photos, I could not help asking her why I had been unable to find any Zehetmeiers in the local cemeteries (I had walked through a lot of them on my own). Exhaling, she took out a few more photos and told us a sad story that answered my question. It was true, there were no Zehetmeier-engraved tombstones in Unterhaching's local cemetery, but more about that in the anecdotes section.

For the next ten years or so, I remained diligent to my new hobby of investigating our genealogy and filling in the blanks between Germany and Kansas. Now that we knew where in Germany they came from, the story took on a new excitement. Now I wanted to know when they had immigrated? What ships they had used to get to America? What ports of entry they had used? Why had they chosen Kansas? I just wanted to learn everything I could about the first generation of Zetmeirs born in America. As happens with most genealogists, the story and the research became both a passion and a hobby during the decades that followed. And like any hobby, it had to take a backseat to our growing family, and my military career. As a result, I found myself putting it down for sometimes years and then picking it back up, to pursue new leads.

As the years passed my family research notebooks gradually swelled to near bursting. As my detective work drew me closer to the present, I grew concerned about respecting the privacy of our living descendants. Not all family stories are humorous anecdotes. As Eva had shown, some leave scars and hurt that go on for a long time. I had long-since met my original goal of finding our family origins in Germany, as well as researching the first two Zetmeir generations born in the United States. So I thought it best to err on the side of caution with regards to researching the living. Now, well over thirty years after I started my genealogy project, I find I am still struggling to find a stopping point. Sadly too, many of our family members who contributed to my initial research have long since passed. And I am a bit sad about not finishing it in time for them to enjoy as well. It is true that a family story never really ends, but at some point, a genealogist must stop and look to putting what has been done into a manuscript as a record for future generations.

In contemplating a format for our family story, I wondered if I should not add some general history as well. I examined and compared several sample genealogies, but they did not include much outside history at all. My concern was that a family tree devoid of some accompanying history might just become a dull ledger of names and birth dates that would not have much character. I wanted readers to feel like they could come to *know* who they were reading about. Sort of like putting some 'historical leaves' on the branches of our family tree, as it were. And our family was especially blessed with several *raconteurs* whose stories and anecdotes, if not included as well, would certainly perish with the passing of time. I did not want that to happen.

I fortunately discovered some published and unpublished historical accounts of others who lived during the Zetmeir times. They certainly help us gain a better insight into the life and times of our family in both Germany and America. I think it gives us a better picture of the events they undoubtedly experienced too. Thankfully, the research also uncovered a few surviving letters written by Joseph and his daughter that are included to add their own words to our story. Research trips in the United States took me through several small towns and county archives in both Kansas and Oklahoma. In 1993, my father and I made a special trip to Buffalo, Oklahoma and ran across some locals who shared land records and directed us to the site of the original Zetmeir homestead. We were thus able to walk the actual ground they had settled on and farmed. And it is funny what geography will do. During our walks, my dad was surprised that he suddenly recalled some long-forgotten childhood stories about his own father and uncles. Several times he would stop and mention some snippet that his dad had told him. Listening and reading about homesteaders of Oklahoma, we gained a greater appreciation of what our family went through to settle this land. It came as no surprise then, that we were very much in sync with the collective American pioneer experience.

So, I have blended both history and family stories from Kansas and Oklahoma into this work. I was particularly elated to find an unpublished account from 1900 written by one of the first families to homestead

Harper County, Oklahoma Territory. Since Joseph Zetmeir arrived in 1901, their experiences must have been identical as to what it took to hack out a living in Western Oklahoma. I struggled with several possible titles for the book, but most seemed either too plain, or too much. As I proofread the manuscript, the thought hit me that if one theme were to characterize our family, it would be "hard work." Then I recalled something my dad used to say, and there it was.

The time is long overdue for me to set down my magnifying glass and put the research thus far collected into an official record. Now at long last, I am at that point. I am confident that this work is complete enough to not only tell the fascinating history of our family, but also to allow both the present and following generations to find their places in our story. And I do apologize for any errors or omissions. For this reason, I have included blank pages at the end of the book. To our present and future family I say only this; your names and stories are just as valuable a part of our collective Zetmeir history as any I have recorded in this book. I simply leave it for you to write.

Leavenworth, Kansas, 2021.

THE HISTORY OF THE ZETMEIR NAME

EVERYONE WHO HAS CARRIED OUR family name would no doubt agree that we all share at least one common thread; we've all suffered the mispronunciations of *Zetmeir* on occasions too numerous to count and its' misspelling on everything from hotel reservations to official records. Which of us has not winced at being called "ZEETmer", "ZETmeer", "ZitMUR", "ZEITmeyer" and countless other mispronunciations during our lives? In my own experience, even the US Army misspelled my last name as "ZETMETER" on my Leave and Earnings statement while thankfully spelling it correctly on my paychecks. So just why is our name so unique and what are its origins?

It's important to recognize right off that our name is unique to and immediately identified with the German state of Bavaria. Upon hearing our name, most any native German will immediately associate it with Bavaria. The other important characteristic of *Zetmeir* is that in its original form, it represented an occupational surname. However, unlike more commonly known occupational surnames such as "Gardner" or "Brewer", ours was still a bit different because it inferred both occupation and the economic status surrounding that occupation all at the same time.

The first part of the name *Zetmeir* derives from the German word for Tithing or tenth part, which is *Zehnt* ("Tsaynt"). The Bavarian version of that was *Zehent* ("*Tsa-hent*"). It is the second part of the name that reveals occupation. In the vernacular Bavarian dialect, farmers were referred to *Mayrs* ("Meyers"). The name could also be spelled "Mayer, Mair, Mayr, Maier, or Meier." In fact, it was not uncommon at all for members of the same family to spell their last names differently using these variations. This would certainly be the case in our family genealogy at least.

So our name is very much tied to Bavaria's history; the common folk could not legally own land, so they worked it through an agreement or contract with a landowner. Hence it evolved that a commoner who farmed a piece of land under an obligation to pay the *Zehent* tithing to a landowner came to be known as a *Zehentmayr*. Thus our name was born. To this day, the name and its varied spellings are still very common in Bavaria. Back when I began researching our genealogy, I did a check of the Munich phone directory in 1984 and found no fewer than seventy-two listings and spellings of *Zehetmeier* in that city alone.

How the actual payment of this *Zehent* tithing itself was conducted is also rather interesting. During the harvest, the *Zehentmayrs* would leave every tenth bundle or stack of produce in the fields for the landowner to collect. The owner, be it the catholic bishop or a nobleman, would then send out their collectors to gather their shares. Collecting this *Zehent* tithing meant ten percent *of each field worked*, not just ten percent of the total yield from the farm itself. Gradually there developed a separate *Zehent* tithing for fruits, beets, kraut, potatoes, wheat, and the other grains. Because there were also other taxes to pay, this arrangement didn't leave much left over for the *Zehentmayrs* themselves.

In cases where the recipient of the *Zehent* was the Catholic Church, it was divided it into thirds among the bishop, the local priest, and the town parish. Over time, it became permissible for landowners to convert their *Zehent* savings into an independent lending institution. Through such methods the church amassed considerable fortunes. The right to collect the *Zehent* on a given piece of property could also be temporarily loaned to another as repayment on a debt, or even simply given as a gift. It wasn't until the year 1848 that a royal decree from the King of Bavaria abolished the *Zehent* laws once and for all.

So how do we go from *Zehetmeier* to *Zetmeir*? The answer to that is as simple as it was common to the immigrant experience in America. Upon arrival at a port of entry, customs officials processing immigrant families most often recorded their family names the way they pronounced it. So they'd often annotate it the way an immigrant pronounced it, or the way they thought it sounded to them. Difficult names were often shortened and simplified by busy or indifferent customs officials. Because immigrants were all fearful of being denied entry, they were not going to argue with them of how their name had been taken down. Likely, a Castle Gardens customs official heard Joseph *Zehetmeier* pronounce his name, and simply wrote it down as it sounded to him. Thus, *Zehetmeier* became shortened to just *Zetmeir*. At least they captured most of the root sounds!

BAVARIA AND THE
THIRTY YEARS WAR

T HE MOST DEVASTATING WAR FOR Bavaria and the towns surrounding Munich where our *Zehetmeier* ancestors lived was the Thirty Years War (1618-1648). This very complex war began as a religious conflict between Catholics and Protestants, but gradually evolved into a political power struggle between France, Denmark and Sweden on one side, and the Austrian and Spanish Hapsburgs on the other. Germany was not a unified country then, but a conglomeration of small principalities (Bavaria being the largest) and was the last remnant of the old Holy Roman Empire. Due to its central location, the war was fought primarily on German territory and has been referred to as the first true "world war." In terms of sheer brutality and destruction, it surpassed even that of many modern wars. It was characterized by marauding armies that lived off the land, extorted the larger cities for ransoms, and generally murdered, pillaged and destroyed everything in their paths as they moved from one region to another. With them came diseases such as typhus, bubonic plague, and scurvy. The pestilence and disease that followed in the wake of the war destroyed an estimated 25% to 40% of the population across the German states. For Bavaria, some estimates range as high as 60%.

Bavaria been largely untouched by the opening phases of the Thirty Years War and had enjoyed relative peace and prosperity. But it became a reality in April 1632 when Swedish King (and new Protestant champion) Gustavus Adolphus invaded Germany and fought his way south to Bavaria. As his plundering army approached Munich on April 17th, he demanded that either an enormous ransom from the Munich city fathers be paid, or else the city would be sacked and burned. Through heavy taxation, the townspeople were to able raise at least part of the demanded Swedish ransom.

With enough of the ransom having been paid, King Aldophus strictly forbade any violence or looting within the city of Munich itself. His orders however, did not apply to the surrounding villages and farms on its outskirts. From their encampment on the *Giesinger Berg*, columns of Swedish soldiers soon began roaming the countryside at will; murdering inhabitants, looting, and burning whatever they could find without regard for human life or property. When caught by surprise, villagers often fled to their village church for protection, hiding their grain beneath the flooring. But most Bavarian farmers had more warning of the approaching columns and quickly packed up their belongings and fled with their families and livestock into the deep forests. A local priest named Father Maurus Friesenegger, who survived the entire war, recorded the villager's plight in his diary; *"The following days will be filled with mournful wailing, fear, and misery. Everyone is busy burying valuables, packing belongings, and fleeing the town. The towns are now totally deserted and the forests are populated."*

The fighting that occurred in Bavaria during the Thirty Years War decimated every town and village surrounding Munich and it's estimated that somewhere between thirty-three to sixty-six percent of the population was lost. The pestilence and diseases that followed in the wake of these marauding armies further reduced their numbers.

NUMBERING SYSTEM

T HE ORDER OF OUR GENEALOGY is arranged using a system that is different from that used on written charts and should make following our line easier to understand. Each person in the family line has both a sequential number and a generation number. For example, our earliest recorded ancestor, Simon Zehetmaier, is assigned the number 1. Then a raised numeral 1 indicating his generation, is placed behind his first name as shown in this example:

"1. Simon[1] Zehetmaier"

Simon's children are then numbered in order of their birth starting with the eldest as number 2, and each of their names are numbered sequentially and with a raised numeral 2, showing they are second, third or fourth child, etc. belonging to the second generation of Zehetmaiers. Each of our direct-line relatives are highlighted in **bold print** and further noted with an asterisk in order to allow the reader to follow our family tree more easily. A paragraph on that direct-line ancestor follows to include their individual stories.

You will notice too that the spelling of the Zetmeir name is vastly different in nearly every family group. I recorded our ancestors using the exact spelling as listed in either German or US records I came across to illustrate the wide variety of spellings our family has used throughout our family history. It is especially important to keep in mind that even when Joseph and Lena came to America, there was no actual "correct" spelling of our surname in the same sense we know it today. So it is not unusual to find a family member listed on a city register as *Zehetmayr*, and then find that very same person listed as *Zehetmaier* on a baptismal record. Joseph's brothers even spelled their last names differently. It is all just part of our story!

GENEALOGY

1. Simon[1] Zehetmaier was born in Keferloh, Bavaria, located just southeast of Munich, around 1600. He is believed to be our earliest recorded ancestor. Because records for this period are not complete he cannot be absolutely confirmed, but an exhaustive search made him the most likely candidate. The sparse information to be found about Simon is that he married a woman named Margaretha in Keferloh, Bavaria around 1620, and they had two children:

2. ***Wolfgang[2] Zehetmayr**   b. abt 1625   d. 17 May 1716
3. Christina[2] Zehetmayr   b. abt 1632

2. Wolfgang[2] Zehetmayr was born in Keferloh sometime around 1625, and married Ursula in 1650/51. Wolfgang was a blacksmith by trade and after having ten children in Keferloh, he and Ursula moved to the town of Poing, just east of Munich. Ursula died in Poing on 4 Jan 1687, and Wolfgang married Barbara Wagner of Hausen on 10 Feb 1687 in the Catholic Church in Anzing. Barbara Zehetmayr died in Poing on 23 May 1720. The Catholic Church death records list her as "the old blacksmith's wife", but no age is given. Wolfgang[2] had ten children by Ursula, and two by his second wife Barbara:

4. Barbara[3] Zehetmayr   b. 15 Jan 1652
5. Wolfgang[3] Zehetmayr   b. 5 Aug 1653
6. Maria[3] Zehetmayr   b. 13 Mar 1656
7. Catharina[3] Zehetmayr   b. 23 Jun 1657   d. 1666/7
8. Johannes[3] Zehetmayr   b. 6 Dec 1660
9. Adam[3] Zehetmayr   b. 18 Apr 1663   d.17 Jul 1679
10. Catharina[3] Zehetmayr   b. 7 Jan 1666

11. Caspar[3] Zehetmayr   b. 25 Sep 1669
12. Elisabetha[3] Zehetmayr   b. 20 Jan 1671
13.***Balthasar**[3] **Zehetmayr**   b. 13 Dec 1672
14. Barbara[3] Zehetmayr   b. 27 Dec 1689
15. Ursula[3] Zehetmayr   b. 27 Sep 1691

13. Balthasar[3] Zehetmayr, son of Wolfgang and Ursula Zehetmayr, was born on 13 Dec 1672 in Keferloh, Bavaria. Balthasar was probably a blacksmith like his father, as it was customary for sons to continue their father's trade. It was also more practical because sons usually inherited their father's tools and trappings. On 28 Jul 1698, Balthasar married the widowed Anna Mayr, whose first husband, Caspar Zellermayr, had died on 8 Jun 1698. They married in Anzing (near Poing), and the ceremony witnesses were; Georg Zellermayr, innkeeper at Pastotten; Caspar Lechner, of Kaisersberg; Balthasar Steidler of Kirchheim; and Martin Lechner, innkeeper at Wifling. It is unknown exactly when Balthasar[3] or Anna died because the burial records in Anzing have a sixteen-year gap between the years 1723 and 1739. They could have died during this period (the most likely possibility), or have simply moved away. Balthasar and Anna had three children:

16. ***Balthasar**[4] **Zehetmayer**   b. 25 Sep 1699   d. 20 Aug 1762
17. Anna[4] Zehetmayer   b. 18 Oct 1702   d. 9 Nov 1702
18. Maria[4] Zehetmayer   b. 11 Feb 1704

16. Balthasar[4] Zehetmayer, son of Balthasar[3] and Anna Mayr, was born in Anzing on 25 Sep 1699. On 7 Feb 1719, he married the widowed Maria Schwaiger and moved to her farm at house number 17, called the *Schmidbartl* (it was common for farms to have both names and numbers), in Unterbiberg and set up a blacksmith trade. Maria Schwaiger died on 3 Aug 1729. Balthasar later married Anna Westiner from Parsdorf, and they continued to live on the *Schmidbartl* farm. In 1758 Balthasar sold his blacksmith equipment, probably due to his older age, or maybe poor health. He died on 20 Aug 1762 in Unterbiberg. Balthasar[4] and Maria Schwaiger had four children:

19. ***Dionysius**[5] **Zehetmayer**   b. 1722   d. 22 Aug 1780
20. Maria[5] Zehetmayer   b. 1725

21. Georg[5] Zehetmayer   b. 1727
22. Wolf[5] Zehetmaier   b. 1729

19. Dionysius[5] Zehetmayer, son of Balthasar[4] and Maria Schwaiger, was born on the *Schmidbartl* farm in Unterbiberg in 1722. Dionysius married Anna Augustin, daughter of neighboring Hans-Georg and Katharina Augustin, on 15 Dec 1761 at the St. George Catholic Church in Unterbiberg. When his father died, Dionysius took over the *Schmidbartl* property and paid his stepmother Anna Westiner, the sum of 200 Guilders. As part of their arrangement Anna had to find somewhere else to live. Ten days later, on 30 Aug 1762, Dionysius sold the *Schmidbartl* and bought the neighboring *Zehetmair* farm (House #10-11) from his father-in-law Hans-Georg Augustin. The *Zehetmair* farm took its name from the Zechetmayer family who had owned it from 1612 to 1628. This period included the Thirty Years War (1618-1648). Dionysius[5] Zehetmayer died on 22 Aug 1780 in Unterbiberg. His widow, Anna, stayed on the *Zehetmair* farm with their children. Anna later married Johann Anton Fuenck of Taufkirchen. When Anna died on 19 Aug 1792, Johann Fuenck paid his stepsons Johann[6] and Dionys[6] 100 Guilders each, thus buying them out of the *Zehetmair* property. Dionysius[5] and Anna had eight children:

23. Anna[6] Zehetmayer	b. 1762/3	d. abt 1781
24. Maria[6] Zehetmayer	b. 1765	
25. Elisabetha[6] Zeh.	b. 13 Jul 1766	d. 5 Apr 1789
26. Theresia[6] Zeh. 1781(abt)	b. 22 Jan 1769	d. 12 Feb
27. Kaspar[6] Zeh.	b. 1 Jan 1771	d. 11 Oct 1772
28. *Johann[6] Zehetmair**	b. 23 Jun 1772	d. abt 1846
29. Dionys[6] Zehetmayer	b. 25 Dec 1774	

28. Johann[6] Zehetmair, son of Dionysius[5] Zehetmayer and Anna Augustin, was born on 23 Jun 1772 at the Zehetmair farm in Unterbiberg. After their step-father bought them out of the *Zehetmair* farm, Johann and his brother Dionys[6] moved south to the town of Unterhaching, where they set up as shopkeepers. The land register of Unterhaching for the years 1808/12 lists Johann[6] as the proprietor of Houses #20 and

#61. House #61 belonged to a local aristocrat named Baron von Zech. It is likely that Dionys[6] lived there and ran the shop under Johann's name.

Johann Zehetmair married Maria Ursula Portenlenger of Unterhaching on 22 Jan 1810, at the Catholic Church in Oberhaching. Johann and Ursula lived at House #20, which was a store (known as a *Kramer*) with a blacksmith shop, and a farm. The landlord was the Catholic Church in Unterhaching. As of this history, House #20 still exists and is still a general goods store just as it was in 1808. Unfortunately, that cannot be said for House #61. During a 1944 bombing raid on Munich, House #61 suffered a direct bomb hit and was completely destroyed. Incidentally, it was the only damaged suffered by Unterhaching during World War II. As of this writing, it is a parking lot for a butcher shop. In 1984, my wife Manuela and I toured the House 20, which was pretty much restored to what it had been when Joseph Zetmeir was born there. The ground floor had only six and a half foot ceilings and there was a fully-equipped blacksmith shop set up in the garage at the back of the house.

Johann Zehetmair died sometime in 1846. The land registry office for that year shows that his son bought the property of House #20 from his widowed mother, Ursula. The 1843 Unterhaching city record lists a *Zehetmaier* as one of the town counselors, but no first name is given. Presuming this office would go to an older man, it is possible it was Johann[6].

Johann and Ursula had only one child, and it is interesting to note that they had their son somewhat late in life; Johann being aged 46, and Ursula 35, having been born in 1783:

29. ***Johann**[7] **Baptist Zehetmayr.** b. 19 Feb 1818   d. 31 Jan 1860

30. Johann[7] Baptist Zehetmayr, son of Johann Zehetmair and Ursula Portenlenger, was born on 19 Feb 1818 at House #20 in Unterhaching. On 9 Sep 1846, he married Katharina Bachmeier, daughter of Alois and Ursula Bachmeier of Feldkirchen, at the Catholic Church in Oberhaching. Johann Baptist bought House #20 from his mother on 25 Aug 1846, and there he worked as a farmer and shopkeeper. The

town suffered an outbreak of Cholera in 1854 which claimed the lives of nineteen of the 417 townspeople of Unterhaching before it ended.

Johann Baptist Zehetmayr died on 31 Jan 1860 of pulmonary consumption following an eight-week illness. Katharina died on 4 Apr 1898, at age 76. Both were buried in the St. Korbinian's Catholic Cemetery in Unterhaching. In 1983, I attempted to locate the Zehetmayr family graves without any success. The story provided by my cousin Eva Barthel explained the rather complicated story as to why our cemetery search had come away without finding any Zehetmayr tombstones.

When Johann[7] and Katharina's oldest son Johann[8] Zehetmayr died of pneumonia on 28 Dec 1895, HIS widow Katharina MAYR remarried the tavern-keeper Paul ADAM who had children of his own. According to Eva Barthel, Paul Adam didn't care for the Zehetmayr's and neither did his daughter Anna Adam, who managed to get her hands on most of their family heirlooms which she promptly threw out. Many years later, Unterhaching decided to consolidate all the town's church cemeteries into one collective city cemetery. A call went out to the town for any living relatives to oversee the disinterment and reburial of their family members in the new central cemetery. Anna Adam claimed the Zehetmayr remains and had them all buried in her family plot, over which she placed a tombstone bearing only her own family name of ADAM. She thus deliberately marked them in obscurity. Eva Barthel related this story to me with great bitterness, even to the point of refusing to let me take a closer look at her only photo of Anna Adam. I suppose every family story must contain a villain!

Johann[7] Baptist and Katharina Bachmeier had six children:

31. Maria[8] Zehetmayr	b. 1847	d. ?
32. Johann[8] Zehetmayr	b. 25 May 1849	d. 28 Dec 1895
33. Michael[8] Zehetmayr	b. 1850	d. ?
34. *Joseph[8] Zehetmeier	b. 14 Feb 1856	d. 26 Oct 1936
35. Anna[8] Zehetmayr	b. 26 Jul 1857	
36. Katharina[8] Zehet.	b. 3 Feb 1859	

34. Joseph[8] Zehetmeier, son of Johann[7] Baptist Zehetmayr and Katharina Bachmeier was born on 14 Feb 1856 at House #20 in Unterhaching. Joseph was only four years old at the time of his father's death. His mother Katharina then married a Simon Mayr around the year 1863 and they moved to Simon's House #6, known as the *Grimmhof*. This was likely a turning point and may be the key reason Joseph Zehetmeier later decided to immigrate to America. Given the laws of inheritance as they then existed, his future in Unterhaching likely did not hold much promise. His original home at House #20 had been sold and, as a stepson living on the *Grimmhof*, he was not legally entitled to any inheritance from his stepfather Simon Mayr. This is probably why he chose to leave Germany for America.

At age 26, Joseph[8] Zehetmeier traveled by train for the northern German port city of Bremen carrying with him a single suitcase. On 14 January 1883 he along with 312 other passengers, boarded the steamship *SS Salier* for the two-week journey across the Atlantic. The ship arrived in New York City on 30 Jan 1883 and Joseph[8] processed through the Castle Garden immigration station. It was likely an immigration official who shortened and recorded his name as *Zetmeir*, because that is how Joseph[8] would write it for the rest of his life.

From New York, he traveled by train to Emporia, Kansas. We don't know what made him choose the destination of Emporia or even the state Kansas for that matter. It was not uncommon for towns to publish advertisements in foreign newspapers extolling the virtues of opportunities to be had to encourage immigrants to come and settle. Perhaps Joseph[8] had seen such an advertisement that made Kansas seem appealing to him. Eleven months after Joseph[8] arrived in America, his future wife came over. On 1 November 1883, Magdalena Stangl, daughter of Joseph and Anna Stangl of Holzkirchen, Bavaria, accompanied by her three-year old daughter Katherina boarded the steamship *SS Hohenstaufen* in Bremen for America. Magdalena and Katharina each had one suitcase. The *Hohenstaufen*'s manifest shows that of 686 passengers that made the voyage, all but one made the voyage in steerage class. During the crossing, five infants died and two more were born. The *SS Hohenstaufen* arrived in Baltimore, Maryland on 17 November 1883.

We do not know exactly how Joseph[8] and Magdalena Stangl met one another, or whether they had known each other before leaving Bavaria. Joseph's village of Unterhaching and Lena's of Holzkirchen are only about 26 miles apart. It is possible and even likely that they met each another in Bavaria. Perhaps they could not afford to marry and come over together and decided that Joseph would go first and send for her once he settled. Some evidence to support this theory is that at that time, single women and children were not allowed to immigrate alone unless they had a relative or sponsor waiting for them in America. But however they met or came to know one another; Joseph[8] *Zecketmeir* and Magdalena *Stangel* (as the church recorded them) were married on 4 February 1884 at the Sacred Hearts Catholic Church in Emporia, Kansas.

Joseph[8] *Setmeir* next appears on the 1885 Emporia city census working as a laborer. A few years later, the 1887/8 Emporia City Directory listed Joseph and Magdalena *Sedmeir* as living at 13 South Constitution Street. Magdalena, who from then on went simply as *Lena*, gave birth to three boys in Emporia between 1884 and 1887; Joseph Jr. John L., and Emil August. Sometime between 1887 and 1892, Joseph moved the family from Emporia to Osage City, Kansas where he found work as a coal miner. On 7 November 1892, Joseph filed a Certificate of Declaration of Intention to become a United States citizen in the district court at the Osage County seat at Lyndon, Kansas. In 1893, they were living at 910 Lang Street, near (Mine) Shaft No. 10. Lena advertised in the Osage City Free Press, offering classes in "Painting and Fancy Work" for $1.50 per class.

KANSAS IN 1883-1900

The decade of 1880-1890, during which time Joseph Zetmeir arrived, the eastern Kansas town of Emporia began to take on some city improvements. In December of 1880, the first gas for street lighting was used. By 1881, even more improvements could be seen; a franchise for a street railway was granted, a telephone company was organized, the waterworks plant was in operation, and a Board of Trade officially organized. A Mr. H. Parkman raised the first crop of Alfalfa grown in Kansas in 1882, and the popularity of this drought-resistant crop soon spread. In 1884, the Ottawa branch of the Santa Fe Railroad was built, thus shortening the distance from Emporia to Kansas City. A branch of the Missouri Pacific Railway was built across northern Lyon County from east to west, and the towns of Allen, Admire, Bushong, and Miller sprang up as a result. Always the town was looking forward to more railroads, and frequent meetings were held to discuss how to attract different railway companies to Emporia.

In December 1885, the first electric lights were installed at a cost of $12.50 a month for private consumption. The town also considered a public sewage system. On July 16, 1885, the cornerstone of the first building of the College of Emporia was laid and thirty-eight acres of land were subsequently donated for the campus. The biggest criminal event of 1885 was the Walkup murder trial, which captivated the interest of the entire state. Mr. J.R. Walkup, a 49 year old widower and long-time Emporia resident, married a Miss Minnie Wallace, age 17, of New Orleans. Shortly after the wedding, Mr. Walkup suddenly died of what was pronounced to be arsenic poisoning. The new Mrs. Walkup was then charged with having administered the drug to him. During the trial however, she was acquitted and soon left Emporia but the controversy divided the community between those who were convinced of her guilt, and those who felt with equal conviction that she was innocent. A Mr. William Jay, a prominent resident, really added to the stir when he formally adopted the young Minnie Walkup as his daughter and threw his money and considerable influence into the fight for her acquittal.

The population of Emporia by 1886 had risen to 9,107 swelling the Lyon County population to 22,819. The first stockyards were built in 1887. There were three daily newspapers in print; the *Emporia Republican, The News,* and *The Globe.* Mule-drawn streetcars transported citizens from east to west between the Katy to the Santa Fe Railroad stations, and from north to south from Normal to Soden's Grove at the end of Commercial Street. Cattle money soon filled Emporia's banks and the county population reached twenty-five thousand people. Free mail delivery was established in July of 1887. The dry summer of 1887 cut short crop yields across the state, and Lyon County soon felt the hard times of depression. In 1890, the annual encampment of the Grand army of the Republic (GAR) brought 5,000 Civil War veterans to Emporia. In that year the first sewer system was installed. Census frauds were charged against the city, asserting that figures were inflated to secure free mail delivery. In July the population of Emporia was authoritatively reset 8,241. This year also saw the first epidemic of a severe form of *La Grippe* (as influenza was called) strike Emporia.

Times got tougher towards the end of the decade too. On April 7, 1892, an 80-mile per hour gale was recorded as the worst storm experienced thus far in southeastern Kansas. Cinch bugs destroyed corn crops, and cattle were dying of Texas fever in Lyon, Chase, and Greenwood counties. The *Republican* was running five columns of delinquent tax lists. The Santa Fe Railroad completed its double tracks to Kansas City. By early 1890, the biggest complaint within the city center was the large number of bicycles on Emporia streets. They frightened horses, caused disastrous horse runaways, and several pedestrians were hit by careless riders. By 1893, rural education took a step forward with the announcement that citizenship rights and duties would henceforth be taught in all district schools. That same year, many Emporia and Lyon County residents made the dash for the opening of the Cherokee Strip in Oklahoma. Many of them did manage to secure land and make that territory their permanent homes. Emporia's most destructive fire occurred in 1893 when the north half of the six hundred block, from Mechanic to Commercial, was burned. The loss was estimated at $75,000.00 and twenty-five horses burned to death in the Barwick livery stable.

The declaration of War on Spain by the US Congress in 1898 saw the raising of Company E of the Twenty-second Regiment, Kansas Volunteer Infantry, in Emporia. Most of the townspeople came to the Santa Fe station to witness the regiment's departure while the 2nd Regiment band played "There'll Be a Hot Time in the Old Town Tonight" and "The Girl I Left Behind Me." The soldiers spent a few weeks in a camp in Topeka, were then sent to Camp Alger, Virginia for the summer. In November, the regiment returned to Emporia from Virginia and was mustered out, having never seen action.

In November 1898 came Emporia's worst economic crisis up to that time; the closing of what had been the town's economic bulwark, the First National Bank. The reports of the bank examiner indicated the bank was in a failing condition. Such was the confidence in the integrity of its officials, however, that investors did not realize the danger in time. Mr. Charles Gross, who was the bank's president, and a son of its founder, committed suicide. The cashier, D.M. Davis, left the United States never to return. Mr. William Martindale, the bank vice-president, turned over everything he possessed, save for his home, to the bank creditors. It was said that he died a heart-broken and disappointed man. Adding to the crisis was the loss of the life savings of hundreds of Emporia's citizens. In many cases, hopes for an old age free from financial worry were ruined overnight. Under the eye of an appointed receiver, the bank occasionally paid out small sums of money to its ever-hopeful depositors. Eventually about sixty percent of the shortage was finally returned to them. For many years thereafter Emporia felt the residual effects of this bank failing. Another casualty was one of the town's newspapers, which had to shut its doors as well. Charles Eskridge, the founder and editor of the *Emporia Republican*, was unable to recoup his losses and subsequently shot himself. By 1899, and somewhat recovered from the bank failure, Emporia held a three-day street fair. This Fair saw the first demonstration in the state of the horseless carriage, forerunner to the modern automobile. The vehicle led the opening of the Fair parade, whose guests of honor included Kansas Governor E.W. Stanley, and a native American Chief from the Pottawatomie Reservation near Topeka.

It was coal mining that had founded Osage City by the Osage Carbon Coal and Mining Company in 1870. The coal mines had brought great numbers of Welsh, Swedish, English, Scots, and Italian, French and German immigrants to the area. In fact, mining companies had for a time offered free railroad transportation from New York City to Osage County in to encourage immigrants to come and work the mines. While the 1870s and 1880s had seen the coal business at its most profitable, by 1886 it had begun to decline when Osage County lost its control of the coal market. That year, the Santa Fe Railroad mining operations moved out of the county as new, richer coal deposits more cost-effective to mine, were discovered to the south in Crawford County, Kansas. While the Missouri Pacific Railroad continued to support mining operations in Osage County, the departure of the Santa Fe Railroad spelled the inevitable end. By 1898, the Santa Fe had disposed of over half its properties and other railroads began reducing their consumption of Osage County coal soon after. Miner's wages had fallen steadily from $2.75 per ton in 1873 to less than half of that in 1893. Miner's wages would continue to fall as Osage County desperately tried to hold on to its coal industry. Wages would not be stabilized however, until the Kansas state government intervened in 1914.

Having initially settled in Emporia and then Osage City, Joseph and Lena Zetmeir had weathered some difficult times in Kansas. But it was a near-tragic accident in the coal mines that led to their decision to leave Kansas for good. The family story passed down has it that 13-year-old Joseph Jr. had pestered his dad for quite some time to be allowed to join him in the mines. Joseph Sr. would not allow it because he thought he was still too young and he himself was losing his enthusiasm for coal mining in general. He was thus very reluctant to see his oldest son in the mines too. But finally one day Joseph relented and agreed to take him to the mines on the condition they would only work as a team. Joe Jr. agreed and the next day off they went one day to work together. In those days, miners carried both their own tools and any shoring materials they needed as well, all of which they pushed in their coal cart. The story goes that the two of them were working a coal vein when old Joseph looked up and saw something about the mine roof that didn't seem right to him. He ordered Joe Jr. to move back with him out of that area of the tunnel. No sooner had the both of them gotten out of there than entire roof suddenly caved in. They had narrowly escaped death or the prospect of being buried alive. Staring at the cave-in, Joseph turned to his son and said he hoped he'd enjoyed his one and only day in the mines because that was going to be the last day he'd ever go into one with him. He is said to have declared; *"That's it, we're not doing this anymore!"* And that was it. Joseph, Sr. never went into another mine again. This was the key event that drove Joseph and Lena to leave Kansas for the Oklahoma Territory soon thereafter.

Their decision to move the family was likely driven by some other economic realities too. By 1900, the Osage City economy had fallen on awfully hard times. They may have considered returning to Emporia, but things were no better there. The largest bank had failed and brought the town to near-ruin. Joseph probably had no prospects back in Emporia. It was well-known that new range lands were available in the Oklahoma Territory. In 1893, the United States government had purchased eight million acres of land in northwest Oklahoma known as the Cherokee Outlet. Though all the best claims had already been staked, there were still homesteads available in the sparsely populated northwest region near the Oklahoma Panhandle. Whether it was the mine accident, or the declining economy, Joseph made up his mind that the next phase of their lives would see them return to what they knew from the old country; they would be farmers again. It was a long way off, but there was at least the opportunity for free land. So, they packed their belongings into a horse-drawn wagon and set out on a 300-mile trek across Kansas for the western Oklahoma prairie. But what would their new world look like?

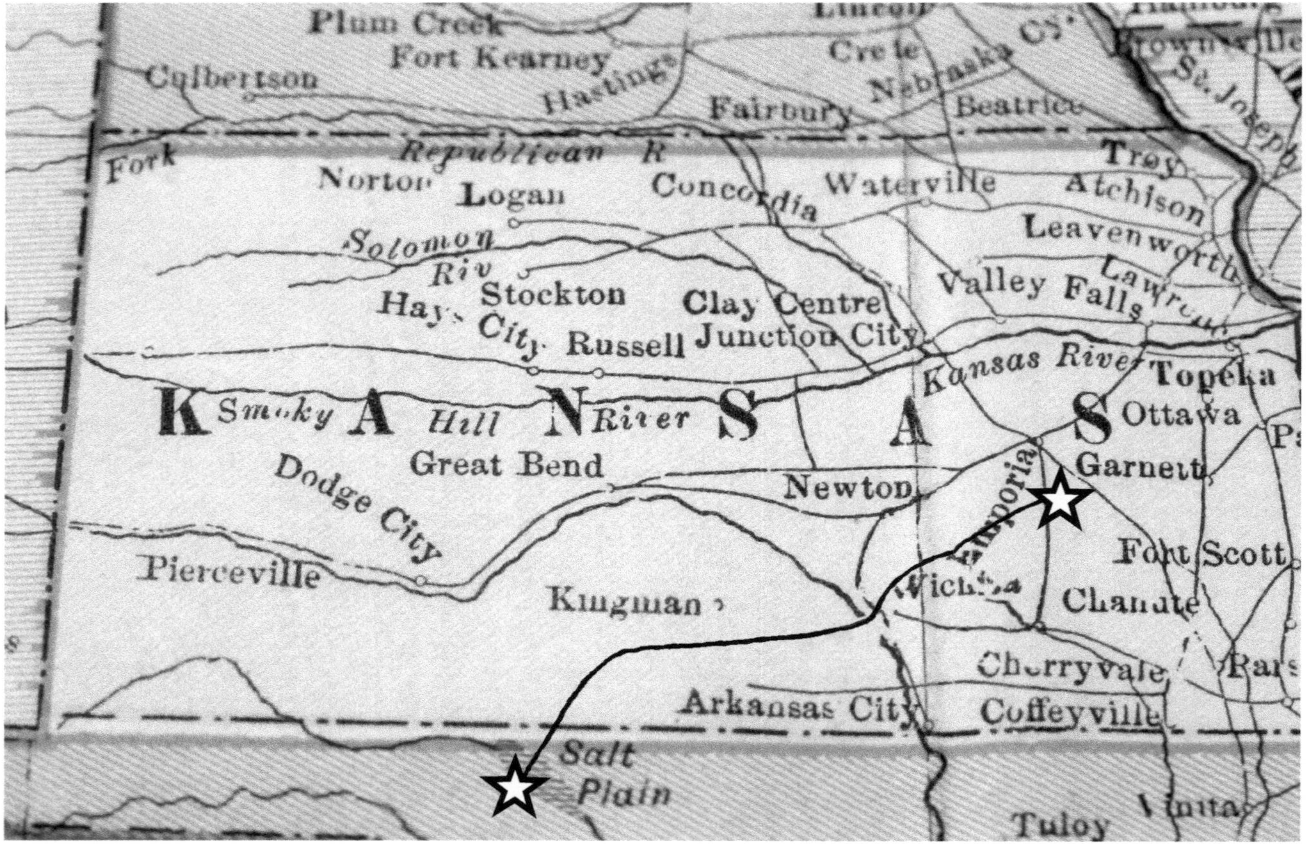
Plum Creek
Fort Kearney
Culbertson
Hastings
Fairbury
Crete
Nebraska Cy.
Beatrice
St. Joseph
Republican R
Fork
Norton
Logan
Concordia
Waterville
Troy
Atchison
Leavenworth
Solomon Riv
Stockton
Hays City
Russell
Clay Centre
Junction City
Valley Falls
Lawrence
Kansas River
Topeka
Ottawa
KANSAS
Smoky Hill River
Great Bend
Newton
Emporia
Garnett
Dodge City
Pierceville
Kingman
Wichita
Fort Scott
Chanute
Cherryvale
Arkansas City
Coffeyville
Salt Plain
Tuloy

OKLAHOMA TERRITORY 1901-1920

The eight million acres of land purchased from the Cherokee Nation and known as the Cherokee Outlet ran from a line north of Tulsa westward across northern Oklahoma to where the panhandle started. Until 1893, it had been used as range land for cattle and was basically a no-man's land. Increasing pressure to open it for settlement though, had finally driven the government to purchase it. On September 16, 1893, the largest and what would be the last major race for land began. Over 100,000 people took part and within a short time, the eastern portion of the Outlet was completed populated. Initially, only a few of the more desirable claims in the western portion of Outlet (present-day Harper County) were settled. By 1900 though, a new influx of homesteaders began to arrive to settle the western lands. These settlers typically would come as a caravan driving wagons with their horses and cattle being herded along behind. It was among this wave of new settlers that Joseph, Lena and their three sons arrived in 1901 to stake out a 160-acre claim near the township of Brule.

Harper County was of course very sparsely populated in 1901. For the most part, it was still a large cattle range. Each of the new homesteaders had cattle of their own that they would turn out to graze alongside those herds from the nearby "Chain C" Ranch. By 1903 however, the cattle were taken off the open range. The nearest post office, store and railroad station was in Ashland, Kansas, about 35 miles to the north. The county seat was in the town of Woodward, located about 45 miles to the southeast. A trip to Ashland and back took a traveler on horseback or by wagon two full days. This was where virtually all the homesteaders purchased their supplies ranging from dry goods to building materials. The newly arrived settlers soon wanted a post office of their own, so a small one was set up in Brule. Anyone within miles around who was going to Ashland would stop by the Brule office to pick up the mailbag to be taken to the post office there. Likewise, they would bring any accumulated mail in Ashland back to Brule on their return trip. The mailman himself would make a mail run to Ashland every other day, so mail arrived on a regular basis three times a week. Even the Kansas City Star newspaper made it all the way out to Brule on a weekly basis. Newspapers were very important to the business of land deals in proving up claims because notices had to be published as a matter of public notice in any newspaper. For a time, each new town even had from one to three newspapers each. When Oklahoma became a state in 1907, the first county seat was established on Henry Miller's farm (Joseph Zetmeir would purchase three town lots from him in 1912) and the township of Brule was renamed Buffalo, Oklahoma.

Western Oklahoma was still a very wild and isolated place. The sand plum was the only native fruit to the area. They grew on bushes about waist high in the sandy soil along streams. They turned very red when ripe and, because they were too sour for much else, they were used for some excellent pies and jellies. These were of great value to the settlers. If settlers didn't have enough jars for canning them, the plums were cooked into a thick batter, and then spread on cloths made from sewn-together flour sacks, and dried until they looked and felt like leather. These sheets of dried plums would then be rolled up and put away for winter consumption. There were also very few trees, save for a few Cottonwoods and occasional Cedars and Elms that grew in the canyons. They were so rare that it was against the law to cut down trees, but they disappeared to become fence posts, barns and houses just the same.

As late as 1900, a few buffalo still roamed and grazed over the territory. Evidence of the vast herds that had existed in the decades before they were hunted to extinction was everywhere to be seen. Bones, horns and the deep muds wallows they'd made to roll in were all over the prairie. There were still no telephones or even a telegraph station in the county. The nearest doctor's office was in Ashland. Very few of the settlers had any money of their own. They relied instead on a barter system, trading butter and eggs for salt, sugar and coffee. A cow or calf might be sold for some needed flour. The first money crops planted were broom corn and wheat. Dust storms and droughts were common since the average annual rainfall was only 18 inches. And there were a great many rattlesnakes to be found. Nearly every settler could recount their regular narrow escapes from being bitten. Deer and antelope were initially plentiful, though these quickly disappeared as the country was settled.

Turkeys and large coveys of prairie chickens could be found among the sagebrush. Of course coyotes were numerous and their mournful howling were heard each night and seen prowling near farmhouses in the early mornings.

Many houses were made of buffalo grass sod. The walls of these "Soddies" as they were called, were about two feet thick. This natural insulation made them quite cool in the summer and yet warm in the winter. The roofs too would sometimes also be covered with sod, or iron sheeting or shingles. Other dwellings were nothing more than cellars or dugouts bored into the side of a hill. Others sod houses were set partially into the ground and were then built up with either sod or boards. Most of these houses only had two or three rooms. Travel was by horse or wagon and there were no roads. Homesteaders going to Ashland or Woodward simply struck out across the prairie. As there were hills and canyons in their way, they had to navigate their way very carefully so as to avoid the deeper canyons and to pass between the larger hills without losing too much distance and travel time. Eventually, these tracks became well-used rutted trails and roads. When going on long trips, people took food and water and simply camped out under the stars as they made their way. When rains hit, rivers and streams might quickly become impassable and require a stay of several days along the banks until the flood subsided.

In late spring there were cattle roundups. The cattle would be driven into a large herds and cowboys would then cut out the unbranded calves and brand them with the same mark as its mother. The cowboys usually wore leather chaps to protect their legs from the brush. They wore large hats and handkerchiefs around their necks as protection from the buffalo gnats and flying ants. Nearly all the cowboys were armed with both pistols and rifles. Nearly everyone went around fully armed. Feuds were rather common and a number of people were killed. Prairie fires were common. Such fires could be frequently seen burning somewhere in the distance. A discarded match or cigarette would start a prairie fire anywhere. In the fall the prairies were completely burned up and were bare as far as the eye could see. Each spring would see the prairies blossoming again with beautiful wildflowers.

The settlers had no churches in the early days. Itinerant preachers passing through the territory would hold meetings and revivals at the school houses. Everyone went to these meetings as they were outstanding events, regardless of the preacher's denomination. There were what people called free or shouting Methodists, regular Methodists, Baptists, and other Christian preachers and they received little or no pay and would stay with different families. The first schools in the territory ran for only three months of twenty days each, there being only sixty school days in a year. A teacher earned about $25.00 a month. One teacher actually received a cow as an incentive for teaching for a fourth month. There were no school books. Each student brought from home whatever books they had brought with them from back east. The teacher would count the books and use the one of which there were the largest number on hand. Spelling, ciphering and geography contests with occasional recitations were the norm.

Life on a claim or ranch was a lonesome existence. It was very common for a homesteading family to go for weeks at a time without seeing anyone else. As new settlers arrived, it was the custom of the country to entertain without charge anyone who might be passing through. It not only afforded them shelter, but also gave the settler news from the outside world. By the time statehood was approved on November 16, 1907, there was a house standing on every good quarter section in Harper County, though some sections were not as good. Overall, times were hard, and the daily trials were many.

This was the world in which Joseph and Lena built their new life. After arriving in Harper Country in 1901, Joseph, Lena and their three sons Joseph Jr., Emil A., and John began the necessities of making their home. Their oldest daughter Katharine had married and remained in Osage City. It must have been a difficult farewell as "Kate" watched her family embark on their journey into the unknown. On 22 April 1901, Joseph filed for his first 160-acre homestead on the 9th Section of 27 Township on Range 22 West, which was located a few miles to the east of Brule. This homestead action was later officially "cancelled by ruling" on 22 September 1901, which means he only held it for about six months. That same month, Joseph filed for a second homestead located a few miles to the south and west of Brule at Section 23, Township 27 North, Range 23 West. This homestead became their family farm for the next several years. On 1 March 1903, Lena gave birth to their daughter Mary F. Zetmeir in Osage City, Kansas. Because the family had moved to Buffalo, Oklahoma by then, it is likely that Lena had taken a train back to Osage City to stay with their daughter Kate to have the baby. A few years later, on 25 Sep 1906, Joseph[8] Zetmeir was granted official United States citizenship by the District Court in Taloga, Dewey County, Oklahoma Territory. He was now officially United States citizen. It would be over a century before another German in the Zetmeir family would apply for US citizenship.

Joseph was well-prepared for this life. He had not only learned farming in Germany, but also blacksmithing and something of the butcher's trade as well. He no doubt kept his three boys busy on the new homestead as they stripped thick sod from the land to build their house, not to mention hauling the materials to add the shingle and iron roof for it. The chores must have been too numerous to count, framing in doors and windows, shoeing horses and mules, building a hen house, gathering the eggs, plowing their 100 acres of arable soil, planting their corn, repairing the farm equipment, mending wagons and harnesses. And the list probably went on from there. The early settlers to Harper County had to take a wagon north to Ashland, Kansas for any supplies they needed, and this was a two-day trip by horse-drawn wagon. Anything that brought in a little extra money was tried. Everyone worked, and everyone contributed their earnings to the family. The three boys soon learned to set out trap lines at nearby creeks to catch racoons for pelts. Joseph bought a hay cutting machine and hired out to other farmers to cut their hay. In 1912, lightning struck their homestead, but the family was able to put it out before serious damage was done. In what seems an uncharacteristic side enterprise, between 1913 and 1916, Joseph and his sons were even managing Buffalo's only roller-skating rink. It was an industrious and enterprising family to be sure! Despite their never-ending workload, the family managed a social life with their fellow townsmen. The Buffalo newspapers mention them repeated in small news clips describing how families visited one another, the local school, or received visitors from out of town. With an initial population in Buffalo of only around 250 inhabitants, everyone came to know everyone else.

By the time Joseph reached age 52, he at last received the official patent on his Brule homestead. The description of his property, dated 6 April 1907, reads in the Testimony of Claimant as: *Prairie land, black soil, best for farming. Upland farm of 160 acres, 100 acres cultivated and 60 acres unfit for cultivation. 70 acres fenced with two wires. Three room sod house, 15x30 ft with shingle and iron roof, sod barn, 15x25 ft, cellar, value 300 dollars. Cropped five seasons, 1902-1906.*

The years of hard work and perseverance had clearly paid off over the years since their arrival on the Panhandle. On 8 June 1908, Joseph paid W.O. Hathaway the sum of twelve hundred dollars for the purchase of an additional 146 acres of land located several miles northwest of Buffalo. This property was recorded as Section 18, Township 28 North, Range 23 West, and was described in the 1910 Harper County agricultural records this way:

ZETMIRE, JOSEPH, Farmer, Buffalo, Settled in County 1901. Native of Germany. Sec. 18, Township. 28 N.,R. 23 W. Upland farm of 146.19 acres. 60 acres cultivated and 50 acres unfit for cultivation. Small orchard. One room frame house. Cave and well.

It is interesting that the deed record for this land transaction shows the title was put into Lena's name and not Joseph's. In April 1912, Joseph purchased even more land; buying town lots #18, #19 and #20 in Buffalo from a William H. Miller (whose farm had served as the first Harper County seat) for the sum of forty-five dollars.

While they were breaking the Oklahoma prairie, the family did manage to correspond with some of Joseph's family back in Germany. Only two letters that evidence this have survived, and both are to Joseph's nephew. In 1914, Joseph answered a letter to his nephew, Johann-Baptist Zehetmayr (from his brother Johann[8] Zehetmayr), who had left Unterhaching to serve in Kaiser Wilhelm II's *Schutztruppe* forces first in China, then in the German colony of *Kamerun* (Cameroon) as a *Polizeimeister*. He had expressed an interest in immigrating to America himself so, in his reply, Joseph described their life in western Oklahoma and offered his advice to Johann this way:

Dear Nephew, I received your postcard, but the letter is very short. Still, I'm glad to hear from you again. You write that you would like to come to America. I am very glad to hear this, but I wouldn't like to see that you later become sorry for this step, to come to the states. First there is the American language. Nevertheless, you could learn this within a few years. Secondly, there is the LAW OF PROHIBITION; no beer, no wine, no brandy. It is very expensive and very bad. Then we have other manners and customs; but you will get accustomed to those very soon. In this country you must pay attention to your things, for the country is full of many lazybones who earn their living by swindle. But you can be on guard and avoid them. Sometimes people can prepare their own beer and wine themselves. Otherwise, the wage is very high here. In winter however, many people are out of work; but those who want to work will always find a job, namely a good butcher who can produce a lot of things can make a lot of money. I can't give you further information for I don't know what you intend to do. In farming I could help you very much, as in butchering, that means with the appliances for the beginning. Other handicrafts, for example a locksmith, cannot be recommended, I think, for all things are made in FACTORIES. Now, I am feeling well. I am not so healthy as before, but I am always content. We live far in the wilderness, but we are settled in very well. Soon we will get a railway, I think. They are always preparing this project. At present our nearest railway* is 18 miles (8 hours) off, two years before it was 34 miles off or about 16 hours. It's getting better and better, isn't it?

Now, are you well? How is your mother and all your brothers and sisters? Tell them they should write to me, too. We have the warmest winter since I have been in America. We had only 2 cold days in February. Last year we had a bad harvest, but this year we expect a good one. I have heard that my brother's (Michael) wife has died; but he didn't write me this, I will say he doesn't write me at all, why not, I don't know. With much love from us I will close this letter and I remain your loving Uncle, with all the best regards from my family.

-Joseph Zehetmeir, Buffalo, OK, 1914.

*The railroad stations Joseph mentions in this letter were in Dunlap, Oklahoma (18 miles away), and Ashland, Kansas (34 miles away).

In an interesting sidenote to our family history, despite his uncle's encouragement, Johann-Baptist Zehetmayr never immigrated to America as they had hoped. The First World War started that same year and it soon engulfed Africa. The British, French and Belgian's own colonial forces soon attacked Kamerun and after an eighteen-month campaign, the surviving German soldiers, Johann among them, conducted a fighting retreat to the neighboring neutral Spanish colony of Rio Muni (Equatorial Africa) where they were all interned by the Spanish on the island of Fernando Po (Malabo). Later they were relocated to internment camps in Spain. When war ended in 1918, Johann was released from internment camp and chose to go back to the now-ex German colony of Cameroon. Our second surviving piece of mail was made in 1922, when Joseph and Lena's youngest daughter Mary wrote to Cousin Johann in Africa from their home in Siloam Springs. She tells about their new life in Arkansas:

July 18, 1922

Dear Cousin,

Several years have passed since we have heard from you, and you will never know how delighted we all were, to hear of you once more. The picture you had sent us of yourself in uniform, we have kept hanging on the wall in a frame, since we received it, and often we looked at it, we said to one another, "he is dead, we will never hear of him anymore", but thank God. You have been spared, and hope that you will from now on, write us more regularly. You are one of us and we would love to hear from you as often as possible, for we all have a warm place in our hearts for you, dear cousin. There sure has been terrible times in Germany and there still are, and how will it all end God only knows. Pappa has been helping Aunt Anna pretty regularly. We have not felt the hard times to amount to anything, of course during the war we were restricted in many things, but we never have went hungry. Pappa has sold our home in Buffalo and also the two farms near it, and we have moved to Siloam Springs, a beautiful little town. It really is a summer resort in the Ozark mountains, and is a great fruit and berry country. In fact, anything we plant grows, and therefore, we have plenty of everything, all kinds of fruit and garden stuff. When we hear from you again, I will send you some codak pictures. I will now close as pappa is writing you all particulars. Hoping that you will answer in the near future, we are your loving folks.

-Mary F. Zetmeir and the rest of the family.

No further correspondence from him has been found. For his military service in World War I, Johann-Baptist Zehetmayr received the Iron Cross, Second Class, the Colonial Badge and a Bavarian Meritorious Service Cross. He died in Bata, Spanish Muni on 31 September 1931 from Blackwater Fever. At his death, local natives looted all his possessions, save one pair of torn trousers.

Joseph and Magdalena lived in Buffalo, Oklahoma until just after 1920, where the Harper County census lists the family as Joseph, Lena and their youngest daughter, Mary. Now aged 64, Joseph sold his properties in Buffalo and the three of them moved to Siloam Springs, Arkansas. There they bought the small house where Joseph would live out his life. It was the first house they had owned in twenty years that was not made of sod.

Joseph and his family had turned from coal mining in Kansas to farming in Oklahoma and had prospered. They had homesteaded the semi-arid Oklahoma plain and had made their farms productive. When Joseph put down his first crop in 1902, the price of wheat was sixty-two cents a bushel. By 1919, World War I had increased the demands for US wheat and had pushed prices to over two dollars a bushel. Most of the farmers in that region prospered handsomely as a result as well. Wheat speculators would soon descend on this region to buy farms wherever they could find them. As it turned out, Joseph and Lena's timing to sell their farms in 1920 coincided perfectly with the market's high demand. But unbeknownst to them, they also narrowly escaped financial disaster as world events were soon to prove. By the mid-1920s, crop prices started declining, forcing Oklahoma farmers to plow more land in order to make the same gains as in previous seasons. It would all be to no avail. The Wall Street Crash of 1929 and the ensuing drought would see most if not all of Joseph and Lena's former neighbors economically ruined. It got so bad that neighboring Beaver County, Oklahoma would become identified as the epicenter of what became known as the "Great Dustbowl" of the Midwest and the Great Depression. The homesteads they had worked so hard to establish became worthless. One can just imagine an elderly Joseph and Lena sitting in their home in Siloam Springs, Arkansas, and giving thanks at their good fortune.

Joseph and Magdalena had four children together: Joseph Jr., John ("Jack"), Emil, and Mary. Katherina had been born in 1881 to Magdalena in Holzkirchen, Bavaria and had come over with her to the United States. As an adult, "Kate" as she was known, adopted her stepfather's name and became a Zetmeir too. Joseph[8] Zetmeir died in Siloam Springs, Arkansas on 26 Oct 1936. He is buried in the Memorial Park Cemetery in Topeka, Kansas. Magdalena later died at their daughter Mary's home in Muskogee, Oklahoma on 17 Jan 1951. Her daughter Katie died a widow in Chicago seven months later.

Katharine Stangl-Zetmeir	b. 23 Jul 1881	d. 5 Jul 1951
35. Joseph[9] Zetmeir	b. 23 Jul 1884	d. 6 Oct 1963
36. John[9] L. Zetmeir	b. Mar 1886	d. Aug 1968
37.*Emil[9] A. Zetmeir	b. 16 Apr 1887	d. 1 Oct 1963
38. Mary[9] F. Zetmeir (Klug)	b. 1 Mar 1903	d Aug 1981

ARKANSAS AND BEYOND: THE FIRST "AMERICAN" GENERATION

JOSEPH AND LENA HAD ESTABLISHED their family very well in America by their retirement years. They had made the long journey from Germany in their youth and had struggled to learn the American way of life and language to a great extent. They had worked extremely hard as common laborers and coal miners in Kansas and had successfully hacked out a living on the Oklahoma prairie, living for twenty years in a sod house to raise their three boys and daughter.

In 1920 Joseph, Lena and their daughter Mary moved to a modest, but comfortable little house in Siloam Springs, Arkansas. After living in a sod house on the Oklahoma prairie for twenty years. One can well imagine that they looked back on all they had been through with no small sense of accomplishment, as well as relief. Relationships within the family were most likely not different from any other. Their children left home, got married, and started their own lives and families. From the few surviving postcards, newspaper announcements and photos, we know they all stayed in touch with one another as best they could. It is also evident that Joseph Sr. also stayed in touch with at least one or two of his own siblings back in Germany, evidenced by his sending money to help his sister Anna following World War I.

We have covered the history of our Zetmeir family from Bavaria to Kansas, Oklahoma and Arkansas. Now we will look at the lives of the first generation of Zetmeirs born in the United States. And from this point on, the generational numbering system used up to this point will stop, as subsequent Zetmeir descendants would end up with parallel numbers. So, what became of Joseph and Magdalena Zetmeir's children: Katherine, Joseph, Jr., Emil A., John, and Mary?

KATHARINE STANGL-ZETMEIR
(MOORE-GARRIGUES-SMITH)

Katharine Stangl Zetmeir, or 'Kate' as she became known to everyone, was something of a family enigma for many years because she moved to Chicago and married a man named Smith. Finding traces of her life were the most challenging of any of our ancestors, and she eventually came to be the author's favorite character to study. The discovery of some old family photos helped answer the many unknowns about her and helped to piece her life together. Katherina Stangl was born in Holzkirchen, Bavaria and made the journey to America with Magdalena when she was only three years old. In Emporia and later Osage City, she grew into a beautiful young woman and in 1898 at age seventeen, she married William Moor of Osage City. Like Kate's stepfather Joseph, Willie also worked in the Osage County coal mines and farmed.

Katie and Willie are presumed to have divorced a few years later. The next record for Katie appears in 1910. That year she married Henry Whitall ("H.W") Garrigues of Camden, New Jersey, in Colorado Springs, Colorado. Henry came from a tool-making family in Camden, New Jersey. Kate and Henry moved to Chicago and took up residence at 1430 E. 6th Street in the South Side of the city. Henry worked in merchandising for the famous Marshall Field & Company department store of Chicago. The 1920 census lists them together with Kate having no occupation on record. Several photos of Katherine show her to be an impeccably dressed and very beautiful young woman. A curious photo shows a clearly older Katherine dressed in a man's business suit and sporting a pipe. This photo could have been taken for either a costume event, or just as a lark. Some photo analysis of the clothing she wore indicates it was likely taken around 1910, when she was still married to Henry Garrigues. The border and size of the photo match another one taken of the man we believe to be Henry Garrigues.

Katie kept in touch with her family back in Kansas and Oklahoma because she sent photos of herself from time to time to her brothers. The Osage City Free Press reported on 28 July 1910:

Mr. and Mrs. Harry Georges (Garrigues) stopped off in this city the latter part of last week on their way to St. Louis from San Francisco. They were the guests of Mrs. Georges brother, Joe Zetmire and other relatives.

This trip supports a formal sitting portrait of Katie around 1910. The Bushnell Studio name is listed on the picture's margin, and Bushnell did maintain a studio in San Francisco, from 1890 to 1920. She and Henry were likely in California on a honeymoon.

Henry and Kate are listed on the 1920 US census as living at 2229 E. 70th Street in Chicago. After 1920 however, her life took a turn for the worse when Henry died unexpectedly on 3 June 1922, while visiting his family back in Camden, New Jersey. When they wrote Henry's obituary, his family did not mention his widow or that he was even married. The next official record on which Kate is found lists her on the death record of what would have been her third husband; Leon S. Smith, of Thomasville, Georgia, who subsequently died on 22 April 1928 in Chicago. This part of her life is a mystery because we leave her in 1920 living with her husband H.W. Garrigues in a middle-class household and then, within the span of the next eight years Henry dies in 1922, Katie remarries Leon, who then dies in 1928 at the age of 22. Katie and Leon lived at 2306 North Clark Street in Chicago near Hyde Park. Leon Smith was twenty-five years junior in age to Katherine. Leon and Katie had not been married for long. On his death certificate, Leon's occupation was listed as waiter, and by this time, the only work Katie found was as a waitress. She is listed on the 1930 US census as a widow living at 480 Forestville Ave, and her occupation is listed as waitress. She is the only Caucasian listed on the census page. By 1940 she lived at 4323 Cottage Grove Ave, and the census notes she is "Unable to work." She marked 'yes' to 'other income sources.' 1940 was the first year the US government started monthly Social Security payments, so this was likely her sole income.

Single and with no formal education, she found herself etching out a meager living as a waitress along with many other independent single working women of Chicago. And it was by no means a kind environment to working women of that era. No doubt her circumstances forced her to steadily sell off the possessions she and Henry had accumulated during their middle-class life together in order to support herself. Waitressing was one of the very few occupations available to single women at that time, and it ranked at the bottom of the societal pyramid. As with most of the single working women in Chicago, her life took a steady descent into poverty.

By 1930, Katherine was living in a low-rent Chicago neighborhood in extremely poor conditions indeed. In 1948, she provided her brother Emil a witness statement so he could obtain a delayed certificate of birth to apply for Social Security. In this statement, she gave her name as "Katharine M. Zetmeir." In 1931, her brother Emil and his nine-year old daughter Doris made a business trip to Chicago where Emil was trying to sell one of his patented inventions to the Santa Fe Railroad. In her only interview with the author, Doris related that while in Chicago, they went to visit Katherine. They were saddened to see her living in such an impoverished state and Doris recalled that Katie had even declined to invite them inside her apartment and had the impression that she did not want them seeing how she lived. Why Katie did not abandon this difficult life and return to live near her parents or with one of her siblings may seem a mystery to us today, but this was a common trait among the breed of fiercely independent, single working women who had cast off from their families and who lived in big cities like Chicago in the early twentieth century. Though they did not have much, they banded together into support groups and while poor, were proud to be on their own and beholden to no one.

In July 1951, Kate's brother Emil Zetmeir in Topeka received a telegram from the Oak Forest Institution Hospital in Chicago that Katherine was a patient and in an extremely sick and frail state. He received a second telegram on 5 July notifying him of his sister's death of heart disease. The telegram informed him that anyone wishing to claim her remains had five days to do so. No one did. Katharine died at age seventy on 5 July 1951, just six months after her mother Lena's death the previous January. Her death certificate listed her occupation as simply 'retired waitress.' She was buried in St. Gabriel's Catholic Cemetery, which served as a Potter's Field for indigent poor Catholic patients who died at Oak Forest Hospital. St. Gabriel Cemetery has no markers on the graves.

Married three times, Kate never had any children. Though hers is one of the most tragic stories in our family history, the photos of her that remain show her to be a woman of great beauty, dignity and humor. She became the author's favorite ancestor to research. And in the end, she proved to be just as tough and independent-minded as any Zetmeir in the family that dug coal or broke the prairie. This 1910 photograph of her taken in San Francisco while in her prime shows her as the lovely woman she most certainly was.

Katharine Stangl Zetmeir, 1881-1951, circa 1910

JOSEPH ZETMEIR, JR.

Joseph Jr. (1884-1963) moved back to Osage City, Kansas where on 5 August 1907, he married Mamie Brady, daughter of Patrick and Susan Brady of Wyandotte County, Kansas. They had three children; Frank, Celia and Joseph "Jody" Zetmeir. Joseph and his brother Emil A. Zetmeir remained close to each other throughout their lives, even dying just a few days apart. Unlike his brothers Emil and John, Joseph did not make the trek to California or Colorado for work. He left the Oklahoma homestead where he grew up to move back to Osage City and Peterton, Kansas, where he remained for the rest of his life. Despite near-fatal mishap he and Joseph had experienced in the mine when he was twelve years old, he returned to coal mining as his occupation. He was well-known as a man with great physical strength. In fact, Joseph earned a reputation as being able to mine, ton for ton, more coal than any of his fellow miners. He also started a dairy farm in Osage City that his son Joseph (Jody) eventually took over. His wife Mamie inherited land from her family, gradually increasing their holdings to around 140 acres. Joseph B. Zetmeir died in Osage City, Kansas on 6 Oct 1963, just five days after his brother Emil passed. Mamie Brady Zetmeir lived on until 9 Nov 1979. They had three children:

Francis P. Zetmeir,   b. 18 Oct 1909   d. 6 Jan 1982.
Celia Zetmeir-Romine,   b. abt 1912   d. abt 1976.
Joseph "Jody" B. Zetmeir, b. 28 Feb 1914   d. 11 Jun 1989.

Frank P. Zetmeir	Celia Zetmeir	Joseph B. Zetmeir ("Jody")
(unmarried)	oo Cecil Romine	oo Opal Allison
		-Dale L.
		oo Georgia Barber
		-Kimberly
		-Brady Dale
		-Janice K.
		oo Michael Brandenberg

"oo" – denotes marriage.

JOHN L. ZETMEIR

John Zetmeir, known to most as "Jack", was born 17 Mar 1886. His baptismal record lists his middle name as "Ludwig", but he often signed his name "John Baptist" during his lifetime. Growing up on the Oklahoma homestead, he also quickly became accustomed the hard work of farming along with his two brothers. In addition to the farm, John worked part-time running a livery stable, a private photographer, and helped manage the family's roller rink in Buffalo as well. Near the Zetmeir farm was the homesteading family of William Norris, who had settled in Buffalo from Christian County, Missouri around the same time. William Norris had eight children, and five of them were daughters. John married one of the Norris daughters, Katie Blanch Norris, and they had two children, a daughter Lena Virginia, and a son, John Thaddeus. John's 1917 Draft Registration card issued in Buffalo contains the notation that he was applying for exemption based of sole support of family. Katie Blanch Zetmeir died of influenza in 1920 while carrying their third child. John later married another Norris daughter, this time Mary Norris-Harmon, who had divorced earlier. They moved to the Merced-Ontario, California area. In 1930 his family was living in San Bernardino, California where John worked as a rancher. His wife Mary died in Ontario on 18 Nov 1952. John remarried Ethel L. who died 3 Dec 1973. John Zetmeir died in San Bernardino on 9 Aug 1968. John and Katie Zetmeir had two children:

Lena Virginia Zetmeir b. 1916 d.?
John Thadius Zetmeir b. 7 Aug 1917, d. 3 Jan 2001

Virginia Lena Zetmeir	John Thadius Zetmeir
oo Gus Doss	oo Olene Hooker (later oo Tom Shirley)
	-Judy
	-John Paul Zetmeir (Shirley)
	oo Janet L. Martin
	-Sandy (Shirley)
	-Shawn

*John T. & Olene divorced. Olene remarried Tom Shirley. Their son, John Paul went by the surname Shirley and did not learn his last name was really Zetmeir until as an adult, he had to produce a birth certificate for the US Army.

"oo" – denotes marriage.

EMIL A. ZETMEIR

37. Emil[9] August Zetmeir, son of Joseph[8] Zetmeir and Magdalena Stangl, was born in Emporia, Kansas on 16 Apr 1887. Like his two brothers, Emil came to know the hard life of homestead farming at an early age. In addition to farming, as a youngster Emil worked for the Atchison, Topeka & Santa Fe Railroad as a so-called "Butcher Boy" that sold small items to passengers during train runs. Everyone in the family was expected to contribute any earnings to the family to make ends meet. Emil and his brother Joseph left Oklahoma for Topeka as the 1907 Topeka city directory lists them both as living at 310 Klein St and working for the AT&SF Railroad. The 1910 Federal Census lists him living back in Buffalo, Oklahoma with Joseph, Lena and his younger sister Mary as a laborer and "home farmer."

On Mar 23, 1913, Emil married Sena May Norris, one of five daughters of nearby homesteader William L. Norris and Virginia Cook, in Buffalo, Oklahoma. Emil and Sena moved to Cressy, California from 1914 to 1917 where they ran a general store. Emil was appointed a US Postmaster on 6 Oct 1914 and his general store served as the post office. From June to August of 1917, Emil also worked as a baggage man for the AT&SF Railroad in Merced. It was in Cressy, California where their first two children, Norris Dean (1914) and Emil A. Jr. (1915) were born. Their first daughter, Della May, was born in Merced on 8 Aug 1917. Shortly thereafter they returned to Buffalo. Emil's 1917 Draft Registration card issued in Buffalo contains the notation that he was turned away for military service because of his family relations living in Germany. Sometime between 1917 and 1920, Emil and his family moved to Walsenburg, Colorado where Emil worked for a coal mine as a superintendent of weights and measures. In 1920 they briefly moved back to Fargo, Oklahoma, where their son Lester Wayne was born. In 1927 they moved back to Kansas; first to Osage City, then Carbondale and later Topeka, where Emil worked as a coach carpenter in the large repair terminal for the AT&SF Railroad.

He and Sena May would spend the rest of their lives in Topeka. When the Crash of 1929 hit and plunged the country into the Great Depression, the bank called the loan on Emil's Topeka house at 628 Sumner Drive. The banking rules of that day allowed banks in trouble to call the loan on a mortgage for the full amount. If owners could not pay, the bank could foreclose. But because of the widespread economic calamity, there was nobody else to buy their house though, the bank allowed him to rent the house. Overnight, and with a family of seven to support, they had gone from being homeowners to tenants. It was the same most everywhere. Fortunately, Emil retained his job with the railroad. His was closest to his oldest brother Joseph Jr., who lived in Osage City as a coal miner, and their families remained close as well and visited one another often.

Though he had only gone to school through the eighth grade, Emil was known for his beautiful penmanship and having an incredibly mathematical and mechanical mind. On the homestead, he had learned carpentry, masonry, some blacksmithing. He was a man who could fix just about anything. During the 1930s Emil attempted to gain patents and market a few inventions. He designed a new type of window sash, and self-sealing baggage door hanger for railroad baggage cars. Though he was eventually awarded a patent, the advent of air conditioning, and metal sash sealed passenger rail cars had rendered his inventions obsolete before they could be adopted. At one point he built several models of his inventions and sent them to the Chicago Utility Company in hopes they were a potential buyer. His models disappeared, leaving him bitterly disappointed. He tried other venues, even traveling to Chicago to find an investor. Despite his many efforts, he never found a backer for his ideas.

By 1950, he had paid off the mortgage on a home at 540 Freeman Avenue in Topeka. Emil Zetmeir eventually retired from the AT&SF Railroad. He died in Topeka, Kansas on 1 Oct 1963. His brother Joseph died five days later. Sena May died on 18 Mar 1965 in Overbrook, Kansas. Emil and Sena May had five children:

Norris[10] L. Zetmeir	b. 21 Apr 1914	d. 26 Jul 1943
Emil[10] August Zetmeir, Jr.	b. 19 Jul 1915	d. 30 Dec 1985
Della[10] May Zetmeir	b. 8 Aug 1917	d. 16 Aug 2010
*Lester[10] Wayne Zetmeir	b. 10 Jun 1920	d. 10 Oct 2005
Doris[10] Ruth Zetmeir	b. 12 Oct 1922	d. 16 Apr 2009

The children and descendants of Emil and Sena May Zetmeir are charted as follows:

"oo" – denotes marriage.

Norris L. Zetmeir	Emil A. Zetmeir	Della May Zetmeir	Les W. Zetmeir	Doris Ruth Zetmeir
oo Helen Dean	**oo Ruth Fairbanks**	**oo William Helm**	**oo Leona Wilson**	**-oo Allen**
-Norris Dean	-Emil F. (Sonny)	-Saundra	-Constance Jean	**-oo Taylor**
oo Opal Marie	oo Sophia Coughlin	oo Jim Branch	oo Huey Frazier	-Kathryn Louise
-Marie	-Ellen	-Laura, -Cynthia	-Debbie, -Lester	**-oo Gardner**
	-Joanie	-Jamma, -Bradley	oo David Laird	**-oo Mieklejohn**
	oo Paul Douglas		-David Jr., -Jodie	
	-Emily, -Abby	-Karolyn	oo Dan Lindsey	
	-Amy	oo Max Butterfield		
	oo Darren Taylor	-Karen, -Annette	-Margaret (Peggy)	
	-Natalie	oo Oren Sharp	oo Robert Varney	
			-Judy	
	-Karl Douglas	-Virginia	oo Chuck Lewis	
	oo Sherrin Coman	oo William Marrier	-Katie	
	-Erik, -Krystyn	-William, -Donna	-Janelle	
	oo Gloria		oo Ashley Fleeman	
			-Kristie, -Becca	
	-Lori		-Jennifer	
	oo Pat Flynn		oo Joshua Richardson	
			-Jordan	
			oo Pete Geier	
			-Les W., Jr.	
			oo Barb Lambert	
			-Jason, -Jillian	
			oo LeAnn Olson	
			-Justin, -Kristen	
			oo Ann Crimbly	
			-Karl David	
			oo Manuela Brümmer	
			-Sonja	
			oo Ryen Shaw	
			-Noah, Henri, Oliver	
			-Virginia	
			-Lori	
			oo Dylan Brown	
			-Jackson	
			-John	
			-Leslie Ann	
			oo Robert Votaw	
			-Robert, Jr., -Alexander	

oo Colleen Merton
-Jacquelyn
oo William
L'Hommedieu
-Austin
-David Michael
oo Oren McClaskey

MARY F. ZETMEIR

Mary Felicia Zetmeir was born on 1 March 1903 in Osage City, Kansas. For a long time, it was thought she was born in Buffalo, on the homestead. Most likely, Lena took the train back to Osage to stay at their daughter Kate's place until she had the baby. Mary came into the world at a lusty fourteen pounds, which may be why Lena chose not to have her on the prairie. As the baby of the family, and sixteen years younger than her closest sibling Emil (born 1887), her relationship with Lena and Joseph was likely especially close. Having a toddler on the homestead must have kept Lena on her toes to keep a close eye on her all the time, lest she find a rattlesnake or get into other mischief. When Joseph and Lena sold out their properties and moved to Siloam Springs, Arkansas, Mary moved with them. She lived at her parents' house until she married. On 10 November 1927 she married William Claude Montgomery in Benton, Arkansas. But it did not last long, and they divorced three years later in 1930. That same year, on 11 May 1930, she married Joseph Klug and they settled in Muskogee, Oklahoma, and later moved to Henryetta. When Joseph died in Siloam Springs in 1936, Magdalena moved to Topeka with Emil, and later settled in with Mary and Joseph, where she lived out the rest of her life until dying in 1951. It was Mary who served as the family witness on their death certificates, taking the time to ensure that their hometowns in Bavaria were included on their death certificates, rather than just 'Germany' as was the case in most documents. This means that the family must have talked about the old country and where they were from enough so that that their children were familiar with Unterhaching and Holzkirchen. The success of this genealogy project is thus due in exceptionally large part to Mary's meticulousness in adding this crucial detail so long ago. We thus owe her a great debt of thanks for this act because without it, finding our genealogy in Germany would have proven nearly impossible. Mary Felicia Zetmeir died in Henryetta, Oklahoma in August 1981. She and Joseph Klug had one child:

Joseph B. Klug b. 1933 (Arkansas)

And so, we come to the stopping point that isn't. The blank pages at the back of the book will allow others to record their own stories. As a possible format example, this narrative of the author's father, Les W. Zetmeir and his family are offered.

42. Lester[10] Wayne Zetmeir, son of Emil August Zetmeir and Sena May Norris, was born in Fargo, Oklahoma on 10 Jun 1920. Les grew up in Topeka, Kansas, where met Lois Leona Wilson at Topeka High School. They married on 3 Nov 1940. Les worked in a meat packing house after they were married and by the outbreak of World War II, he was working for the AT&SF Railroad as a blacksmith's helper in their huge repair shop in Topeka.

In 1943, Les enlisted in the US Merchant Marine and received basic seamanship training at the US Maritime Service Training Center in St. Petersburg, Florida. He found sunny Florida both beautiful and exhilarating compared with Topeka. Part of his basic seamanship training included a two-week cruise of the Gulf of Mexico aboard the three-masted training Barkentine, the *Joseph Conrad*. Climbing masts, knotting lines and learning old school seamanship was the adventure of a lifetime for Les. He enjoyed it so much he somehow finagled an arrangement to draw another two-week trip out on the *Conrad* in place of other scheduled training. He would fondly talk about this time for the rest of his life. Certified as a deck hand, he was sent to Sheepshead Bay, New York for specialty training as a Pharmacist's Mate. For the rest of the war, he worked out of New York's Brooklyn Army Base as a deckhand aboard tugboats for the Moran Towing Company. Aboard their tugs he made trips up and down the entire eastern seaboard, towing barges loaded with cargo and assisting shipping. German U-boats had begun sinking enormous amounts of US shipping in early 1942 in what became known as the Battle of the Atlantic. One of their jobs then was assisting and towing to shore ships that had been struck by torpedoes off the coast. New York City provided both excitement and a fast education for a man from Kansas. Leona and their daughter Connie eventually joined him in New York City.

After the war, Les returned to Topeka where he learned the floor covering trade working for J.C. McCormick Company. Following that, he went to Los Alamos, New Mexico to do contract work on the US Army base at White Sands. No doubt recalling the beautiful white beaches and palm trees of his training in St. Petersburg, he and Leona moved to Madeira Beach, Florida where he bought and managed four small efficiency apartments. This business endeavor ultimately proved unsuccessful. In 1955, Les and Leona divorced, and he moved to Kansas City, Missouri, to work for his brother Emil. Lester and Leona had three children:

44. Constance[11] (Connie) Jean Zetmeir   b. 27 Nov 1942
45. Margaret[11] Elain (Peggy) Zetmeir   b. 9 Jan 1946
46. Lester[11] W. Zetmeir, Jr.   b. 12 Sep 1948

In 1956, Les[10] Zetmeir married Ann Crimbly, daughter of Italian immigrants Amedeo Ciarimboli and Virginia Baroni, who had immigrated before World War I from Colleferro, Italy to South Greensburg, Pennsylvania. Les and Ann married in Winchester, West Virginia. They lived in Kansas City, Missouri where Les resumed the floor covering trade. He and partner L.E. Charles started Grandview Linoleum & Tile Company in Grandview, Missouri. Afterwards, Les opened his own floor covering business called Northside Floors in Kansas City (North), Missouri. In 1962, Ann was diagnosed with cancer and died on 20 Dec 1962. Les[10] and Ann Zetmeir had two children:

47. ***Karl[11] David Zetmeir**   b. 22 Jun 1958
48. Leslie[11] Ann Zetmeir   b. 2 Jul 1960

Les[10] married Colleen J. Cypert-Merton of Stillwater, Oklahoma on 30 Nov 1963. Back troubles eventually forced Les to give up the floor covering business and he took a sales manager position for Kansas City Bolt, Nut & Screw Company. In his fifties, he teamed up with Warner Case and Ed Rush as business partners and together they formed Case Supply Company. He retired as their Sales Manager in the 1980s. Colleen worked for Wheeling Steel, Inc. in Lenexa, Kansas. Colleen had two children from her previous marriage to Jack Merten. Les adopted both of Colleen's children, who later changed their names to Zetmeir:

Jacquelyn Joy Zetmeir   b. 16 Oct 1948
David Michael Zetmeir   b. 2 Oct 1950   d. 6 Jun 67

FAMILY ANECDOTES

Storytelling is very much a Zetmeir family trait. I continually pestered my dad to tell us of the times "when he was little" and he would always recount a funny story or two for us. Some of the stories were funny, while others just more reflective of the times back then. In any case, I cherish them all.

Neither Joseph nor Magdalena ever learned to speak English very well. In fact, I cannot recall ever hearing Grandpa Joseph ever speaking at all. -Della May Helm (1917-2010).

As a boy, my dad worked for the railroad as a "Butcher Boy." He told me old Joseph would meet him at the train stop with a bullwhip in one hand, and the other hand outstretched to collect whatever money he had earned. -Les W. Zetmeir (1920-2005).

The Zehetmayr men were all known to be somewhat quiet, but with explosive tempers. –Eva Zehetmair-Barthel, Germany, 1984.

A friend of my dad's (Emil A.) ran into him in downtown Buffalo one day and told him he had better stay away from the local pool hall because his brother Joseph (1884-1963) was in there 'getting the hell kicked out of him.' Emil ran to the pool hall only to find Joseph standing in the middle of the floor with a pool cue in his hands and everybody else stretched out cold on the floor. -Les W. Zetmeir (1920-2005).

There are no Zehetmeier gravestones to be found in Unterhaching cemeteries. The reason is a family feud. Joseph Zetmeir's older brother

Johann was first married to a woman named Katharina Mayr. When Johann died in 1895, Katharina remarried a man with the surname ADAM, who apparently hated the Zehetmayrs. He had a daughter named Anna Adam who must have hated them too, because she threw out or sold off most of their family possessions. When the St. Korbinian cemetery was to be emptied in the 1920s, townsfolk were called to oversee the exhumation and reburial of their relatives. Anna had all the Zehetmayrs reburied in her ADAM family plot, under her name only. So bitter was this event that as our cousin Eva Barthel explained the story to me in 1984, she got furious all over again. She even refused to give me a copy of the one photo she had of Anna Adam, or even let me hold it. She told us not to even look at it. -Karl Zetmeir, (1958 -)

My brother Emil (Emil A. Jr. 1915-1985) and I were in the woods one day just sitting on an old log. Without warning, Emil up and smacked me across the head, sending me falling backwards. I came back up ready to fight when he pointed at the ground. There was a big snake moving where my feet had been. He said he was afraid if he had warned about the snake, I might have startled it and been bitten, so knocking me off the log seemed the logical thing to do. -Les W. Zetmeir (1920-2005).

My dad (Emil A.) told of how his brother-in-law Bill Wildhaber would go into Buffalo every day and pay a dime to get a shave. He said a man too lazy to shave himself is not of any account.

−Les W. Zetmeir (1920-2005).

One day while helping me to lay floor tile in my kitchen Dad told me this story of when he was a journeyman in the floor covering business. Dad did not believe in unions. One day he was on a job laying floor tile when he looked up to find himself surrounded by his co-workers. "Les, it's time for you to join the union". Dad stood up and said, "well, I know I can whip any of you two at a time and some of you three at a time, but I can't whip twelve at a time, so I'll join. Though he signed up Dad always swore that he never paid a dime into the Union.

-Leslie Ann Zetmeir-Votaw (1960-)

My brother Emil and I were in his car one day when we got pulled over. Emil suddenly realized he had left his wallet at home. In those days we looked a lot alike, so I slipped him my drivers license instead. After the officer wrote the ticket and left, I kidded him about who the hell forgets their wallet? He handed me the ticket and said: "I believe this is yours." -Les W. Zetmeir (1920-2005).

My sister Doris and I used to go dancing together on weekends. She was a great dancer, but she always managed to pick a fight with someone, and I would have to fight our way out of there. -Les W. Zetmeir (1920-2005).

I went to Chicago with my dad to see Aunt Kate when I was nine. I do not remember seeing any husband, I only remember she was living kind of poorly and did not want to let us inside. –Doris Ruth Zetmeir (1923-2009).

Mary Klug was a different lady, she dressed strangely with her hair all wadded up in two big knots on her head. We took her to the bus station after a visit once. –Doris Ruth Zetmeir (1923-2009).

As a teen, our dad was quite an athlete; basketball, football, table tennis, and he especially loved tennis. He told the story of how he had worked odd jobs and saved ten dollars to buy a new a new tennis racket. When he bought it home, he never forgot the look his father (Emil, 1887-1963) gave him for spending the equivalent of a week's groceries for the family, on a tennis racquet. -Karl David Zetmeir, (1958-).

My dad (Emil A. Jr. 1915-1985) and I would drive down to Muskogee and visit my Aunt Mary (Klug). He had me measure her kitchen for some new cabinets and he would always leave her some money. -Emil F. "Sonny" Zetmeir (1941-2013).

Dad (Emil F. "Sonny Zetmeir) was teasing the kids in the yard. He scooped up a small tree frog and pretended to eat it, declaring it tasted like a pickle. My mom's best friend and next-door neighbor came around the corner in time to see the last tip of a little frog's leg passing her 4-year daughter's lips. She didn't talk to my dad for a few years."

-Ellen Zetmeir

I had a paper route when I was a kid. There was this man who never paid me though. He would always tell me he had put the money in his mailbox. I stopped throwing his paper. One day I passed his house when he was outside lying in his hammock. He called out; "Hey, where's my paper?" I yelled back: "I put it in the mailbox, where you keep your money!" Later, I went back and saw he was asleep, so I dumped him out of his hammock and ran away. -Les W. Zetmeir (1920-2005).

Dad played marbles as a kid and took a lot of pride in his ability. I was visiting Dad's sister May (she was in her late 80's) and I mentioned what a great marble player Dad had been. Suddenly Aunt May's eyes opened wide, she sat straight up, pointed her finger at me and said, "I WAS THE MARBLE PLAYER OF THE FAMILY and I could BEAT YOUR DAD!!" -Leslie Ann Zetmeir-Votaw (1960-)

While working in New York City (during his time in the Merchant Marines) Dad pitched softball for money on a team of Italian dock workers. They called him the "Kansas City Kid". -Leslie Ann Zetmeir-Votaw (1960-)

Every NYC dock was both ethnic and had a softball team. Dad was hired onto the "Italian" dock because he could fast pitch softball. His tugboat skipper would use his arm to throw the "monkey fist", a small lead ball wrapped in twine on a thin cord that was thrown up and over the sides of ships so they could pull over a hawser to rig a tow. One day dad threw the monkey fist as hard as he could to clear the side of a large Norwegian freighter. Just as he let it fly, a sailor stuck his head over the side and the "fist" hit him squarely in the forehead. Dad said he heard the guy falling down a ladder and feared he had killed him. But a few minutes later, he reappeared and, in a thick Norwegian accent, called out: "Iss dat ALL?" -Karl David Zetmeir, (1958-).

As a kid Dad would play hooky from school and hang out in the rotunda at the top of the Capitol Building in Topeka, KS.

-Leslie Ann Zetmeir-Votaw (1960-).

Dad hated all the squirrels they had and used to shoot them with a .22 rifle. Mom would not let him shoot them when the "little girls" were visiting. One morning at the breakfast table we saw his rifle barrel sticking out from the corner of the house. Then *BAM*. We all cheered when we realized he got two squirrels with one shot. Went right through one into the other." -Joanie Zetmeir-Douglas.

Dad really felt the stigma of having had to wear overalls to school, which back then was a symbol of poverty. I learned this when I came home from college wearing a pair of overalls. To him, it meant that you were literally from the wrong side of the tracks in the railroad town of Topeka, KS. -Leslie Ann Zetmeir-Votaw (1960-)

Whenever ships or boats collided, it had to be reported to the harbor master as an accident. There was a tug captain named Frank that always seemed to be running his boat into something. One day he called-in yet another accident and the harbor master exploded back over the radio: "Jesus H. Christ Frank, you've hit everything in the harbor but an airplane, what in hell's name have you hit now?!" In truth, Frank had run his tug into a seaplane that was tied up at a pier. -Les W. Zetmeir, (1920-2005).

As a young boy, 'Pawdy' (Joseph Zetmeir, Jr. 1884-1963) would set traps along the nearby creek to catch Possums or Raccoons. He would follow his trap line on the way to school and if he had caught something, he would take it back home to skin and clean it. If his traps were empty, he would just go onto school. Once a month, the farrier, who they called "the hide man", would come around to buy pelts. The day he came around, none of the town boys could be found in school. –Dale L. Zetmeir, (1946 –)

FAMILY ANECDOTES

Aunt May's husband Bill Helm was the kindest, nicest man you would ever know. One day while working for Montgomery Ward in Topeka, he noticed a customer walking a bicycle towards the back of the store. Bill was only too glad to open the back door for him and wish him a nice day on his way out. A few minutes later, the Manager came running up. The man had stolen the bicycle. -Les W. Zetmeir (1920-2005).

When I was about 12, my family attended an Easter sunrise church service, held at a nearby park. It was an overcast, cold windy and rainy day and the congregation were all dressed in black, dark grey or brown colored coats. Everyone sat on picnic tables under a large shelter, waiting for the pastor to arrive. I was seated between my parents. Soon a car pulled up and out stepped the pastor; wearing a bright banana-yellow leisure suit. My dad muttered aloud; "I guess we can start now, the EASTER BUNNY is here." I couldn't stop laughing, despite my mom pinching my leg to keep quiet. As soon as I'd stop, I'd look up at my dad, he'd wink at me, and I'd crack up all over again. My mom nearly pinched my leg black and blue. -Karl David Zetmeir (1958-).

The German Empire - 1871

Joseph Zehetmeier's birthplace of Unterhaching; just south of Munich.
Magdalena Stangl's birthplace of Holzkirchen is further south.

FAMILY PHOTOS

Earliest known Zetmeir document. The baptismal record of Balthasar
Wolfgang Zehetmayr, 1672, Keferloh, Bavaria.

Das Zehetmair: Dionysius[5] Zehetmayer (1722-1780) bought this farm in
Unterbiberg, from Hans-Georg Augustin. The name is from the *Zechetmayer*
family who owned it from 1612 to 1628. It was demolished in 1902.

House #20, Unterhaching, (1934). Johann-Baptist Zehetmayr (1818-1860) and Joseph Zetmeir (1854-1936) were born here.

House #6, The *Grimmhof,* Unterhaching. Joseph Zehetmeier left this home for America.

Joseph Zetmeir's parents. Johann-Baptist Zehetmayr, 1818-1860, and Katharina Bachmeier, 1824-1898.

Zehetmayr cousins reunion, Hohenschaeftlarn, Bavaria,1984. Eva Zehetmayr-Bartel (center) who tracked down the author in 1984 and was vital to forging this story. Author's wife Manuela and daughter Sonja at far right.

Herr Weisse, owner of House #20, Unterhaching, at the blacksmith forge that was part of the property since Joseph Zehetmeier lived there.

SS Salier. Ship on which Joseph Zehetmeier arrived in New York 30 Jan 1883.

Magdalena Stangl and three-year old Katharina arrived in Baltimore aboard the
SS Hohenstaufen (right), 17 Nov1883.

First photos of Zetmeirs in America, circa 1887. Taken at Traders in Emporia, Kansas. Joseph, Magdalena Zetmeir, Katharina, John L., Joseph Jr. (Magdalena appears to be pregnant.)

Emporia, circa 1889. L to R: Joseph Jr., Joseph, Katharina (Katie), John, EmMagdalena Katharina, John, Lena, Emil.

Prairie Homestead, Buffalo, Oklahoma circa 1906. Lena Zetmeir and daughter
Mary. *"Unser Häusl" (Our house)* is penciled on the back of the original.
Note the dugout hen house and plow on right.

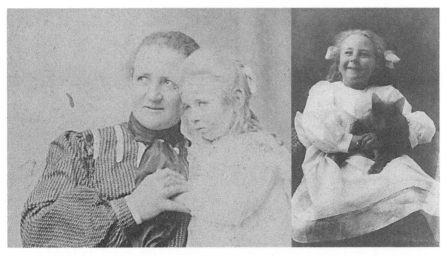

Lena and Mary Zetmeir (Klug). Born in 1903, Mary was the baby of the family and
sixteen years younger than her closest sibling, Emil (1887). Her relationship with
Lena and Joseph was no doubt close.

Harvesting peanuts, Buffalo, Oklahoma circa 1903-1915. The Xs on each indicate family members. Joseph and his family no doubt celebrated this bounty.

John "Jack" Zetmeir (1886-1968) in 1967.

Emil A. Zetmeir (1887-1963).

Emil A.& Sena May Zetmeir, 1913.

Mary F. Zetmeir, circa 1905.

Norris L. Zetmeir, & "Mrs. Wink", circa 1915

Mary Norris (L.) would be John L. Zetmeir's second wife. Sena May Norris (R). married Emil A. Zetmeir

Les W. Zetmeir, (1920-2005) on the site of the original Zetmeir Homestead, 1993. The town of Buffalo is in the background.

John "Jack" Zetmeir (Center), unnamed location. Jack worked around horses all his life, so this could've been taken in Buffalo, Fargo, or California.

Emil A. & Sena May Zetmeir with the author (left) and sister Leslie (right), circa 1961.

The United States of America

IN THE DISTRICT COURT OF THE

Sixth Judicial District of Oklahoma.

In and for Dewey County, Sitting with the Powers of a District and a Circuit Court, of the United States of America.

Be it Remembered, That at a term of the above entitled Court begun and held in and for said County, in Taloga therein, on the _3 5_ day of _Sept_ in the year of our Lord One thousand Nine Hundred and _2d_ , present the Honorable J. L. PANCOAST, sole presiding judge, _J. A. Mathis_ Sheriff of said County, and IRA A. HILL Clerk of said Court, the following among other proceedings were had and done, to-wit: _Joseph Jelinor_ a native of _Germany_ and at present residing in said Territory, appeared in open Court, and made application to be admitted to become

A Citizen of the United States.

And it appearing to the satisfaction of the Court that he had declared on oath before _Clerk District Court_ _of Saguache county, Col._ a court of record having common law jurisdiction and using a seal, two years at least before his admission, that it was bona fide his intention to become a citizen of the United States, and to renounce forever all allegiance to any foreign Prince, Potentate, State or Sovereignty whatsoever, and particularly to _The Emperor of Germany_ of whom he was heretofore a subject. And said applicant having declared on oath before said Court, that he will support the Constitution of the United States and that he doth absolutely and entirely renounce and abjure all allegiance and fidelity to every foreign Prince, Potentate, State or Sovereignty whatsoever, and particularly to the Power above named, and that he does not disbelieve in and is not opposed to all or any organized government; that he is not a member of or affiliated with any organization entertaining or teaching such belief in or opposition to all or any organized government; that he does not advocate or teach the duty, necessity or propriety of the unlawful assaulting or killing of any officer or officers either of specific individuals or of officers generally of the Government of the United States or of any other organized government because of his or their official character, and that he has not violated and will not violate any of the provisions of Chapter 1012 of the Act of Congress approved March 3, 1903, entitled "An Act to regulate the immigration of aliens into the United States." And the said Court having made careful inquiry into all of these matters and caused to be entered of record the affidavit of the said _Joseph Jelinor_ and his witnesses _Robert Young_ and _Henry White_ in reference thereto, and being satisfied that the said applicant has resided within the United States for the term of more than five years next preceding his admission, without being at any time during the said five years out of the territory of the United States and within this Territory more than one year.

And it further appearing to the satisfaction of this Court that during said time he has behaved as a man of good moral character, attached to the principles of the Constitution of the United States, and well disposed to the good order and happiness of the same

It is Therefore Ordered by the Court, That the said _Joseph Jelinor_ be and is hereby admitted to become a citizen of the United States.

In Testimony Whereof, I, Ira A. Hill, Clerk of the Court aforesaid, have hereunto set my hand and affixed the seal of said Court at my office in the City of Taloga, in said County of Dewey, and Territory of Oklahoma, this _2 5_ day of _September_ A. D. 190 _6_

Ira A. Hill
_____
Clerk of the District Court.

By _R V Brownlee_ Deputy.

Final Certificate No. **4104**

4—196.

Application No. 18781

HOMESTEAD.

Department of the Interior,

UNITED STATES LAND OFFICE,

Woodward, Oklahoma,

November, 19, 190690

It is hereby certified *That, pursuant to the provisions of Section No. 2291,*

Revised Statutes of the United States, Joseph Zetmeir,

has made payment in full for

SE¼,

of Section No. 23, *in Township No.* 27 N. , *of*

Range No. 23 W. , *of the* Indian *Principal*

Meridian Oklahoma, *containing* 160 acres.

Now, therefore, be it known, That on presentation of this certificate to the

COMMISSIONER OF THE GENERAL LAND OFFICE, *the said* Joseph Zetmeir,

shall be entitled to a patent for the tract of land

above described.

Register.

Final deed to Joseph Zetmeirs homestead, 1906.

79

Christmas on the Homestead.
Mary Felicia Zetmeir (Klug)

Magdalena "Lena" Zetmeir
raised three sons and a daughter
on the Oklahoma prairie.

With older brother John as a
photographer, Mary Zetmeir no doubt
became a favorite model.

"Hold that pose…"
John L. "Jack" Zetmeir,1886-1968

Katie (1881-1951) married William Moore in 1989 in Osage City at age 17.

Mary Felicia Zetmeir (1903-1981) circa 1919.

The three Zetmeir brothers (L to R): Joseph, Jr. (1884-1963), John "Jack" (1886-1968), Emil August (1887-1963).

Katharina "Katie" Stangl-Zetmeir as a teen in Osage City, Kansas (left). She stayed in Kansas.

Kate Zetmeir-Garrigues in Chicago, circa 1915. Photo taken at Hyde Park Studios.

Henry Garrigues (left) and Kate were married in Colorado in 1910.

"Katie" Zetmeir (1881-1951) was the most enigmatic of the family to research. Married three times and widowed twice, she lived out her life on her own terms in Chicago.

Johann-Baptist Zehetmayr (1883-1931).
Joseph Zetmeirs nephew with whom he
corresponded about coming to America. After
mandatory service (1903-1907), he joined the
colonial *Schutztruppe* in Peking, China (1907-
1909). The photo (right) from China is the
one Mary said in her letter that hung in their
house. He returned to Germany in 1909. In
1914 he joined the *Polizeitruppe* in Kamerun.
In WWI, the Germans fought their way to
Spain's neutral colony of Spanish Muni and in
1916 were interned (below). Here they have
surrendered to a Spanish officer (center). The
German colonial Governor, Dr. Ebermaier, is
the bearded man in the straw hat (front).

L to R: Mary, Lena & Joseph at their home in Siloam Springs, Arkansas.

Lena sitting with photos of Kate and Harry Garrigues – mourning?

Lena, Emil, Mary Zetmeir-Klug, circa late 1940s.

Mamie Brady Zetmeir & Joseph Zetmeir

Joseph L., Mamie, daughter Celia, Emil
& Sena May Zetmeir

Emil & Sena May Zetmeir, sons Norris
(1914-1943) & Emil (1915-1989).

Emil Zetmeir & Sena May
23 Mar 1913.

he 'Super' watching t
+ Trip

e 'Super' going ofte
The Trip

he Trip coming out

Emil Zetmeir (1887-1963) as Superintendent of weights & measures,
Walsenburg, Colorado

Her Majesty and
the Flivver

This is in the Sun
if you can tell wh
I was sick all day.

Sena May driving their "Flivver" and (r.) with her sister Rosella Norris-
Wildhaber

88

Emil Zetmeir & Sena May Norris
wedding photo 23 Mar 1913.

Emil & Sena May Zetmeir, 1940.

Emil and Sena May Zetmeir with baby Norris, in their General Store,
Merced, California, circa 1914 (unknown customer at left).

John Zetmeir (1886-1968).
First wife Katie Norris (1898-1920)
on left. His second wife, Mary
Norris (1928-1952) above.

Joseph Zehetmeier, born
Unterhaching, Bavaria, 1856. Died in
Siloam Springs, Arkansas, 1936.

Magdalena Stangl-Zetmeir, born
Holzkirchen, Bavaria, 1864. Died in
Muskogee, Oklahoma, 1951.

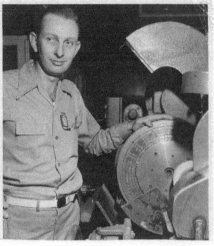

Emil A. Zetmeir, Jr. (1915-1985)

Norris Dean Zetmeir (1914-1943)

Della May Zetmeir –Helm, (1917-2010)

Lester Wayne Zetmeir
(1920-2005)

Les, Della May, Emil, Sr., Sena May, and Emil, Jr. Zetmeir

Les, Ruth (Fairbanks), Emil, Colleen (Cypert) Zetmeir

Les Zetmeir & Leona Wilson   Les Zetmeir & Ann Crimbly

Doris Ruth Zetmeir (1923-2009)

William Helm & Della May Zetmeir Helm   Norris Dean & Emil A. Jr. Zetmeir, circa 1916

628 Sumner, Topeka, Kansas. Home where Emil & Sena raised their five
children: Norris, Emil, Della May, Les, and Doris.
The author (r.) and father Les Zetmeir (l.) pictured in 1988.

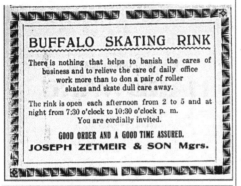

BUFFALO SKATING RINK

There is nothing that helps to banish the cares of
business and to relieve the care of daily office
work more than to don a pair of roller
skates and skate dull care away.

The rink is open each afternoon from 2 to 5 and at
night from 7:30 o'clock to 10:30 o'clock p. m.
You are cordially invited.

GOOD ORDER AND A GOOD TIME ASSURED.

JOSEPH ZETMEIR & SON Mgrs.

r County Journal (Buffalo) 29 Jan 1915

Notice in this issue the ad of the
skating rink. D. M. Neatherly
and Harry Williams have purchase(
the rink from Mr. Zetmeir.

o Republican, 12 Oct 1916

During the storm last Thursday night. lightning struck the
Joseph Zetmeir home. southwest
of town. Quick work soon put
out the fire before any heavy
damage resulted.

We enjoyed a heavy rain last
Thursday night and another lib-
eral downpour on Friday night.
Considerable wind accompanied
the storm, but no great amount
of damage is reported.

gle, 9 May 1912

From: Former Buffalo Girl

The following stanzas were written by Miss
Mary Zetmeir, daughter of Mr. & Mrs.
Joseph Zetmeir, of Siloam Springs, Ark., but
who lived in Harper county until four years
ago. This was sent to Mrs. Ervin VanDorn.

"MY OLD CHILDHOOD HOME"

Out upon the lone prairie many years ago,
My father took a claim and many crops did
sow;
We built a house of sod and trusted in our
God.
As far as one could see there was not a single
tree.
Water it was scarce, for out upon the plains,
Many a time we were badly in need of rains.
Many a night we heard the wild rangers
stampeding,
And found in the morning that all our crops
they had been eating.
Sad and lonely, feeling so blue; Often we
looked to the East.
And thought of our loves ones, too. For of
hope there seemed not the least.
As I grew older, I learned to love those old
sand hills. And watch the cowboys drive the
cattle through the rills.
Often I climbed the canyons steep,
to watch the men harvest reap.
As time sped on, things took a change,
And when one looks back it seems so
strange, For where the old sod house once
stood; Now stands a modern house of wood.
Nice smooth roads lead here and there,
And all the land has been fenced with care.
Pretty towns have sprung up everywhere
And they make one think of the times when
"Things looked bare."
There are no more rides in the old ox cart;
You now look for the railroad chart.
The rain has come and made things grow.
And now it is "Hurrah for the town of
Buffalo."

13 March 1924, Buffalo Republican

Joseph Zetmeir, who is mowing hay on the Maxwell place, came to town the other day for repairs and left his machine in the meadow. During his absence some thief or miscreant removed one of the wheels from the mower and it cannot be found. This is a mighty small piece of business as the mower is now practically worthless and was almost a new machine.— Mighty small potatoes!

Buffalo Bugle – 1911.

We understand that Mr Zetmeir, who resides South of Buffalo, has the agency for a patented Device for butter making. In the patent it is Evident that Mr Zetmeir has a money maker Better than a gold mine. The machine is adapted In the making of butter out of clabber milk. The Operator takes one pound of butter and five Pounds of clabber milk, puts these into a receptacle And after three minutes churning takes out six Pounds of the finest butter you ever looked upon. The product looks like butter, smells like butter and tastes like butter and in fact is butter until About the third day after manufacture and then is When the purchaser and this particular brand of Butter fall out. If the pure food law can be compiled right we will look for some wonderful progress in the manufacture of "boarding-house butter" in this Section and Mr Zetmeir will not be able to handle The immense orders for his devise. -22 April 1910

Married at the home of the bride's parents on Ninth street, Wednesday, April 20, 1898, by Squire Swartwout, William Moor to Katie Zetmire, only daughter of Mr. and Mrs. Joseph Zethmire. The young couple are well known in Osage City and their many friends wish them a long and happy life.

Wedding Bells.

Married, at the home of the bride's parents, north of Buffalo, last Sunday evening at 8 o'clock, Miss May Norris and Emil A. Zetmeir, two of our well-known young people.

The nuptial ceremony was performed by Elder J. G. McNutt in the presence of only the immediate relatives. The attendants were John Zetmeir and Miss Mary Norris, brother and sister of the contracting parties.

The bride is the daughter of Mr. and Mrs. W. L. Norris and the groom is the son of Mr. and Mrs. Joseph Zetmeir. The happy couple have a large circle of friends in this community with whom we join in congratulations and wishes for a long, happy and prosperous future.

2

Mr. and Mrs. Harry Georges stopped off in this city the latter part of last week on their way to St. Lious from San Francisco. They were the guests of Mrs George's brother, Joe Zetmire and other relatives.

Notice in this issue the ad of the skating rink. D. M. Neatherly and Harry Williams have purchased the rink from Mr. Zetmeir.

Republican, 12 Oct 1916

John Zetmeir and wife are the proud parents of a fine baby girl, born to them Wednesday morning of this week. Mother and babe are doing fine, and some hopes of the father's recovery. At first we feared he would lose his mind, he acted so queer, he would go out of doors and run around the house seven times a minute making an awful noise. At last it was discovered that he was trying to get used to the sound of papa, then the ladies that were there talked to him, and told him that he would soon get used to that, so he seems pretty well reconciled.

rnal (Buffalo), 29 Oct 1915

Only a Joke

Last week we published, upon the request of Mr John Morrison, of south of Buffalo, a little piece in regard to a butter making device, of which Mr Zetmeir has a sample. The article was written in the spirit of a joke and were of the opinion that the substance of the article was a little joke between Mr Morrison and Mr Zetmeir. Perhaps we erred, but in doing so we simply complied with the request of Mr Morrison. Thinking that the Morrison and Zetmeir families were friends, and that the matter was a little joke between them, we published the story as to us and as requested, never dreaming that it would occasion any hard feelings. However we stand corrected and desire to apologize to the Zetmeir family for any part for which we are responsible. No better people reside in this community than the Zetmeirs and the last thing we would do would be to intentionally offend them or discredit them. We are informed by Mrs Zetmeir that most of the substance of the article is untrue, the device mentioned being for the merging of one pint of sweet milk and one pound of butter for home consumption. No sour milk is used and as a money saver in the home the device is a valuable one. -29 April 1910

BIBLIOGRAPHY

BOOKS

Donovan, Frances K. (2012) The Woman Who Waits, Forgotten Books. (1920) Boston: Gorham Press, Richard Badger.

Egan, Timothy (2006) The Worst Hard Time. New York: Mariner Books.

Esslinger, Dean R. (1988), Forgotten Doors, The Other Ports of Entry to the United States. Philadelphia: Balch Institute Press.

Felzmann, Rudolf (1983) Unterhaching: Ein Heimatbuch [Unterhaching: A Home Book]. Im Selbstverlag der Gemeinde Unterhaching, Landkreis München.

Graudenz, K., Schindler, H. (1984) Deutsche Kolonial-Geschichte [German Colonial History]. Südwest Verlag; München.

Hall, Clayton Coleman, (1912) Baltimore Its History and Its People, New York: Lewis Historical Publishing Company.

Hobmair, Karl, (1979), Hachinger Heimatbuch, München: Seitz Druck GmbH.

Menzel, Heinrich (1936), Harper County Oklahoma Platt Books of 1910 (1995), Die Kämpfe in Kamerun ("The Battle for Kamerun"), Berlin: Junker und Dünnhaupt Verlag.

Meyerowitz, Joanne J. (1988) Women Adrift: Independent Wage Earners in Chicago, 1880-1930. Chicago: University of Chicago Press.

Peacock, John (1993),20th Century Fashion, New York: Thames and Hudson, Inc.

Taylor, Maureen A., (2013) Family Photo Detective, Cincinnati, Ohio: Family Tree Books.

Westin, Jeane E. (1977) Finding Your Roots. Los Angeles: J.P. Tarcher, Inc.

CHURCH RECORDS

Catholic Parish Records, St. Stephan, Oberhaching, Bavaria, Germany for years 1783, 1810, 1818, 1846.

Sacred Hearts Catholic Church, Emporia, Kansas. Marriage Records for Joseph and Magdalena Zetmeir, Record of Baptism for Joseph, Jr. and Emil August Zetmeir (1887)

GERMAN SOURCES

Administrative Landcourt of Wolfratshausen, Bavaria. Auszug aus den Briefprotokollen des Pfleggerrichts Wolfratshausen Familie Zehetmayer. BR1322/89, BR1324/104, BR1326/108, BR1319/80, BR1322/89.

Archiv für Ahnenforschung des Erzbistums München, Birth Records for Magdalena Stangl, marriage & death records of her parents, Joseph and Anna Stangl.

Holzkirchen Standesamt, Holzkirchen City Civil Records. Birth record for Katharina Stangl, 1881.

Statsarchiv München, Kataster Nr.13 877, *Liquidation des Besitzstandes zugleich Grundsteuer Kataster, Ortschaft Unterhaching, Haus #20.*

Ship Photos provided by Hapag-Lloyd AG, Werbeabteilung, Ballindamm 25 Hamburg, Germany.

GOVERNMENT SOURCES

Department of Vital Statistics
Arkansas – Death Certificates of Joseph & Magdalena Zetmeir
Illinois – Death Certificates of Katherine Zetmeir-Smith
Kansas – Death Certificates of Emil & Joseph, Jr. Zetmeir
Oklahoma – Birth and death certificates

Cook County Archives, FHL 1892131. Death entry for Leon S. Smith, husband of Catherine Zetmeir.

Census records for Osage City, Kansas 1885 & 1890.

Census records for Emporia, 978.162, 1887/1888.

Harper County Oklahoma Platt Books of 1910 (1995), pages 41 (27N 23W) & 53 (28N 23W).

Kansas State Census, Lyon County, Emporia, 1885, p. 39.

National Archives Microfilm Publications. Ship's Manifest for S.S. Salier, 30 Jan 1883.

National Archives Microfilm Publications. Ship's Manifest for S.S. Hohenstaufen, 17 Nov 1883.

National Archives Census records, 1900-1940.

National Archives, Homestead Claim and Final Approval for Joseph Zetmeir, Homestead Land Records for Woodward County, Oklahoma Territory, Record Group 49, File 4104.

NEWSPAPERS (VIA NEWSPAPERS.COM)

Osage City Free Press, (1898) Marriage announcement of Katherine Zetmeir and William Moor, p. 28.

Harper County Journal (encompasses the former Buffalo Bugle, Buffalo Democrat) 1910-1916.

Muskogee Daily Phoenix, 18 Jan 1951, Obituary for Lena Zetmeir

PUBLISHED MANUSCRIPTS

French, Laura M. (1929) History of Emporia and Lyon County. Emporia: Emporia Gazette Print.

Hartsock, D.L., (1971). The Impact of the Railroads on Coal Mining in Osage County 1869-1910. Kansas Historical Quarterly, 37(4), 429-440.

Harper, Roscoe E., (1938), Homesteading in Northwestern Oklahoma Territory. Chronicles of Oklahoma,16(3), 326-336.

Railroads in Oklahoma, 1870-1974. (1976), University of Oklahoma
   Press.

Dewey County Historical Society, (1976), Spanning the River, Vol I.

UNPUBLISHED MANUSCRIPTS

Rousch, K. Coal Mines of Osage City, Unpublished manuscript.

South Suburban Genealogical and Historical Society, (2010), Hazelcrest,
   Illinois. Oak Forest Hospital Cemetery.

YOUR STORY

YOUR STORY

YOUR STORY

YOUR STORY

YOUR STORY